DATE DUE

BRODART, CO.   Cat. No. 23-221

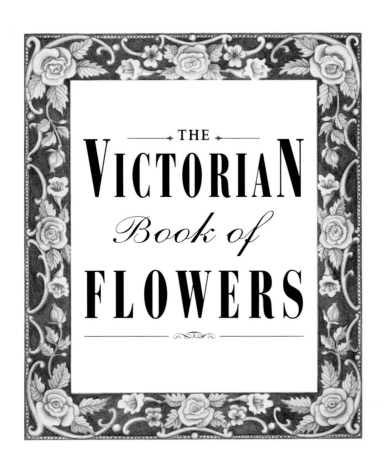

THE
VICTORIAN
Book of
FLOWERS

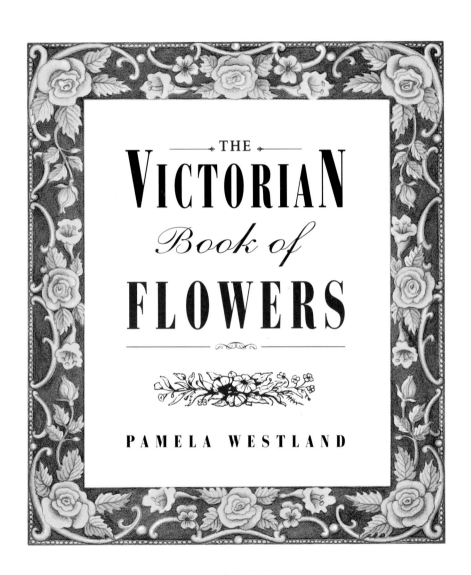

THE

VICTORIAN

Book of

FLOWERS

PAMELA WESTLAND

SMITHMARK

Designed and created by

THE BRIDGEWATER BOOK COMPANY

DESIGNER *Peter Laws*

ART DIRECTOR *Annie Moss*

EDITOR *Joanne Jessop*

MANAGING EDITOR *Anna Clarkson*

PHOTOGRAPHER *Nelson Hargreaves*

PAGE MAKE-UP *Chris Lanaway*

CLB 4084
© 1995 CLB Publishing

This edition published in 1995 by
SMITHMARK Publishers,
a division of US Media Holdings, Inc.,
16 East 32nd Street, New York, NY 10016

SMITHMARK books are available for bulk purchase for
sales, promotion, and premium use. For details,
write or call the manager of special sales,
SMITHMARK Publishers,
16 East 32nd Street, New York,
NY 10016 (212)-532-6600

Produced by CLB Publishing
Godalming Business Centre
Woolsack Way, Godalming, Surrey, UK

ISBN 0-8317-7292-1

Printed in Singapore

10 9 8 7 6 5 4 3 2 1

FLOWERS IN THE VICTORIAN ERA

Introduction

As we turn back the clock on the Victorian era, we find a preoccupation with the use of flowers that is perhaps without equal. The Victorians turned to flowers for their visual and aesthetic pleasures in decorating and scenting their homes, in the preparation of beauty products and simple medicines, in cookery and most of all in their romantic liaisons.

In this book, we show how our Victorian ancestors turned to the delightful language of flowers to convey their innermost thoughts to their loved ones. With the diffidence of shy young suitors and the coyness of pretty young maidens in mind, we have composed decorative and meaningful bouquets that pose and answer the most intimate of questions.

The Victorian appreciation of flowers began at an early age. We discuss how a child's first love, for his or her mother, could be expressed in the simplest and prettiest of ways, in a hand-arranged posy or a cluster of fresh meadow flowers to touch the heart.

Looking back in fascination at the Victorians' preference for strong, rich colours when furnishing and decorating their homes, we have composed pot-pourri blends and seasonal floral arrangements that would have perfectly complemented those vibrant surroundings. A basket of lavender and rosebuds, a ring of pressed pansies, a wreath of blue-going-on-purple cottage-garden plants and herbs, a rosebud pomander, a pyramid of richly coloured dried flowers, and romantic bedside posies – all these designs are unashamedly laced with pure nostalgia.

The Victorian royal household instituted a new fashion in Christmas celebrations and decorations that soon became fashionable on both sides of the Atlantic. Their contribution is extensively acknowledged and some traditional Christmas ideas are developed in pages devoted to the joy of giving and receiving, and all the fun associated with yuletide festivities.

Wander round a garden plucking a few leaves here and a few flowers there and, like our Victorian ancestors, you can utilize them to make gentle, soothing and beautifying products for your own dressing-table. There are recipes for rosewater marigold lotion, camomile shampoo, and other beauty aids.

As you turn the pages of this book, we hope that it will evoke, for you, all the glamour and romance of Valentines and love posies, the scent of lavender and the beauty of lace – the charming feast of flowers and fragrances beloved by the Victorians.

CONTENTS

PART ONE

The

Flowers & Foliage of

Spring

In the Spring, when young Victorians' fancy turned to thoughts of love, couples would celebrate their shared joy with an exchange of meaningful message posies and floral Valentine tokens. Demure ladies could exploit in both culinary and artistic ways the symbolism of pansies, for thoughts, and sweet violets, for modesty. Spring was a time of burgeoning flowers and blossoming love.

THE LANGUAGE OF LOVE

Will You Be Mine?

orget-me-not, heart's ease, love-in-a-mist, love-lies-bleeding – sometimes the popular name of a flower implied a sentiment too tender or too painful to be expressed in words between shy Victorian lovers. But the opportunities for meaningful declarations of love or heartbreak did not stop there. The language of flora, which had been handed down from one generation to another and is formalized in a number of Victorian dictionaries, offered the tongue-tied suitor and his belle a rich and colourful way of conveying their innermost thoughts and secret longings – of saying it with flowers.

A young man on his way home from church might offer a blushing maiden a bluebell plucked from the wayside as a signal of his constancy, a white clover flower to implore her, 'Think of me,' or a spray of purple lilac to indicate that he was experiencing 'the first stirring of love'.

With access to a garden, the young suitor could widen significantly his floral vocabulary. He might proffer an iris to signify that he had a message, then present a ranunculus to convey his message: 'You are rich in attractions.' Adding more colour to his token and weight to his sentiments, he might add a red tulip as a declaration of love and, boldly, a jonquil to make the unequivocal statement, 'I desire a return of affections.'

Single flowers and message posies were not always passed from hand to hand; a relationship might be too tender for that, or the opportunities for a meeting too remote. A posy might be left beside a garden gate, in the branch of a tree or concealed in a basket of vegetables sent in from the kitchen garden.

But when a flower was handed to the loved one, then there were further shades of meaning to be understood and observed. If a flower was inclined to the right the pronoun 'I' was implied, whereas inclining it to the left implied 'thou'. If a flower was touched lightly to the head it signified distress, and to the bosom listlessness. A red rose could convey more than just true love. If the stem was stripped of its thorns it was a sign of fear; if the stem was also stripped of its leaves, the despairing message was 'All hope is lost.'

RANUNCULUS
You are rich in attractions

IRIS
I have a message for you

TULIP
A declaration of love

JONQUIL
I desire a return of affections

THE LANGUAGE OF FLOWERS

The Answer is Yes!

Victorian maidens, wishing to signify their acquiescence in love, must have had as much difficulty in composing a nosegay as in writing a letter. The inclusion of a certain flower or leaf could be as revealing as the written word, giving the recipient as much reason to hope or despair.

A red carnation meant 'My heart is affected.' A rose leaf, 'You may hope.' A clutch of daisies, 'I share your sentiments.' A ring of lords and ladies (pulmonaria), 'We will be together.' And then the tantalizing decision – to put them in, or throw them away – a few blades of grass, which symbolized the ultimate, 'Submission'.

A coquettish miss might tease her young beau with marjoram flowers, for blushes, a stem of London pride, signifying frivolity, or a crimson polyanthus flower to make him ponder on 'the heart's mystery'. Unwanted attentions could be brushed aside with a single flower, a yellow tulip to indicate hopeless love or, more forthrightly, wild liquorice, which makes the uncompromising statement 'I declare against you.'

Composing a 'yes' posy

1 Hold the central flower, a carnation, in one hand and arrange the small flowers, lords and ladies, around it. Add blades of grass and rose leaves and bind the stems.

2 Bind on the small cluster of daisies and tie the stems with a ribbon. Even at this stage, it is not too late to pull out the grass (for submission) if you change your mind.

Extracts from a Victorian dictionary

Flower	Meaning
AFRICAN MARIGOLD	vulgar minds
ALYSSUM, SWEET	worth beyond beauty
ANEMONE	forsaken
BACHELOR'S BUTTON	celibacy
BALSAM, RED	touch me not
CALCEOLARIA	I offer you my fortune
CARNATION, YELLOW	disdain
CHRISTMAS ROSE	relieve my anxiety
CLOVER, FOUR-LEAVED	be mine
COWSLIP	winning grace
CROCUS	cheerfulness
CUCKOO PINT	ardour
DAFFODIL	chivalry
FENNEL	love of praise
FOXGLOVE	insincerity
FURZE	love for all seasons
GERANIUM	gentility
GILLYFLOWER	unfading beauty
GOLDEN ROD	encouraging
HOLLY	am I forgotten?
ICE PLANT	your looks freeze me
JASMINE	transport of joy
LADY'S MANTLE	fashion
LADY'S SLIPPER	fickleness
LAURUSTINUS	a token
LILY, DAY	coquetry
LILY-OF-THE-VALLEY	a return of happiness
LOVE-IN-A-MIST	perplexity
MAIDENHAIR FERN	discretion
MARIGOLD	grief, despair, prediction
MINT	virtue
NASTURTIUM	patriotism
OATS	witching soul of music
ORANGE BLOSSOM	your purity equals your loveliness
OX-EYE DAISY	patience
PEA, EVERLASTING	an appointed meeting
PERIWINKLE	pleasant memories
PETUNIA	your presence soothes me
PINK, RED DOUBLE	pure and ardent love
PRIMROSE	early youth
PRIMROSE, EVENING	inconstancy
RAGGED ROBIN	wit
RHODODENDRON	danger, beware
RUE	disdain
SAGE	domestic virtues
SHEPHERD'S PURSE	I offer you my all
SNAPDRAGON	presumption
STRAW	broken engagement
SWEET PEA	delicate pleasures
VALERIAN	accommodating disposition
VERONICA	faithfulness
VIOLET, WHITE	modesty
VIRGINIA CREEPER	I cling to you forever
WALLFLOWER	fidelity in misfortune
WAX PLANT	susceptibility
WHEAT STALK	prosperity
YARROW	solace
YEW	sadness

This array of spring flowers forms a
natural link between home and garden.

FLORAL COMPOSITIONS
Open Wide the Windows

After the rich deep greens and reds of winter, the Victorians welcomed spring with a profusion of blossom and flowers gathered from the garden or garnered on a country walk.

While daffodils and tulips, cherry, apple and pear blossoms were fashioned into arrangements for the dining-room and drawing-room, floral compositions for the morning-room were more natural-looking and free. This was where the lady of the house might sit to write her letters or plan her guest lists, and where her daughters might choose to read or do their embroidery.

There might be a lustre jug of primroses or cowslips on a writing table, or a deep blue bowl of hyacinths in an alcove. A collection of white or cream pottery jugs clustered together on a table close to an open window might be filled with a profusion of flowers in colours that, in themselves, heralded spring. Pale yellow and deep golden daffodil, thick trusses of white and mauve lilac, spires of lemon-yellow forsythia and pollen-rich twigs of furry pussy willow formed a natural link between house and garden.

Groups of flowering plants added colour and variety to the scene; pink, yellow, red and white ranunculus, purple, blue and pink auricula, and primulas in colours from morning gold to sunset pink made the morning-room a cheerful place to be in the spring.

A DAY IN THE COUNTRY

The New Broom

A walk in the countryside in Victorian times was all the more rewarding for the first sight of the new season's broom, with its bright sunshine-yellow flowers. Broom, which favours dry downs, sandy pastures, heaths and wastelands, was recognized not only as a harbinger of spring but also as a versatile ingredient in the kitchen.

The honey-like sweetness of the flowers and buds make them especially suitable for use in desserts, though they have a long history as a colourful salad ingredient. Pickled broom buds (preserved in white wine vinegar flavoured with mustard seeds) were a favourite with the Victorians. The flowers were also used to flavour syrup for fruit salads and candied as cake decorations.

Always pull off the green calycles when using broom in any culinary way. They have a sharp, bitter flavour.

Asparagus and broom salad

Asparagus and broom salad

— SERVES 4 —

Serve this delightful salad as a first course, or as part of a cold buffet meal.

YOU WILL NEED

- 675 g (1½ lb) asparagus spears, trimmed
- 1 small carrot, trimmed and thinly sliced
- 15 ml (1 tbsp) seedless raisins
- broom flowers
- 30 ml (2 tbsp) olive oil
- 15 ml (1 tbsp) white wine vinegar
- a pinch of mustard powder
- salt and pepper

❖ Lightly poach the asparagus in boiling, salted water until it is just tender. Drain the spears, plunge them into cold water to prevent further cooking, then drain them again. Pat the spears dry with kitchen paper.

❖ Arrange the asparagus in a wheel pattern on a flat serving plate and scatter the carrot and raisins over them. Place the broom flowers around and in the centre of the dish.

❖ Mix together the olive oil, wine vinegar and mustard, then season the dressing with salt and pepper. Just before serving, pour the dressing over the salad.

Baked broom custards

SERVES 4

The delicate flavour of the broom is intensified with honey in this turn-of-the-century dessert.

YOU WILL NEED

❖ 25 g (1 oz) butter
❖ 30 ml (2 tbsp) cornflour
❖ 300 ml (½ pint) single cream
❖ 30 ml (2 tbsp) set honey
❖ 3 egg yolks
❖ 40 g (1½ oz) ground almonds
❖ 60 ml (4 tbsp) broom flowers, trimmed, plus extra for decoration
❖ 30 ml (2 tbsp) caster sugar

❖ Preheat the oven to 200°C/400°F/gas 6.
❖ Melt the butter in a small pan over medium heat. Add the cornflour and cook for 2 minutes, stirring constantly. Mix in the cream and stir continuously until the sauce thickens. Stir in the honey.
❖ Remove the pan from the heat and beat in the egg yolks one at a time. Stir in the ground almonds and broom flowers, then divide the mixture between four individual ramekin dishes.
❖ Sprinkle the tops with caster sugar and stand the dishes in a baking dish with 2.5 cm (1 in) of water. Bake for 20 minutes.
❖ Decorate the tops with individual broom flowers or sprays of flowers and serve hot.

Baked broom custards

NAME CALLING

The Latin name of the plant, *Cystisus scoparius*, may not have a romantic ring to it, but some of its country names do. And one, *bizzom*, has close associations with the household utensil.

Some of the regional variations on the name include *banadle*, *bennel*, *basam*, *bizzom*, *cat's peas*, *common broom*, *golden chair*, *green broom*, *green wood*, *lady's slipper* and *scobe* or *scobie*.

And its meaning?

In the Victorian language of flowers, broom signified neatness, humility and ardour.

HEDGEROW SPARKLE

In the Spring Sunshine

As the spring sunshine gathers strength and hedgerows give off the heady smell of grapes, it is time to do what our Victorian ancestors loved to do – make elderflower 'champagne'. The huge creamy-white clusters of flowers that hang like perfumed umbrellas along country lanes, and in some gardens too, were endearingly known to Victorian children as 'bread and cheese'.

To their parents, the flowers signified zealousness; an eagerness, perhaps, to sit on a shady lawn listening to the click-clack of croquet balls and sipping glasses of the sparkling drink whose only intoxicating element is its deliciously sweet-going-on-tangy flavour, and its aura of luxury.

This upper-income-bracket aura is not founded on reality. All you need to make the golden yellow country drink with the champagne image, besides water and the flowers themselves, is sugar, lemons and vinegar. Use more or less sugar than that specified in the recipe, according to taste.

The sweet smell of success

Gooseberry and elderflower water ice; strawberries macerated in elderflower syrup; elderflower fritters served with whipped cream and brandy, and Muscatel raisins soaked in elderflower vinegar – the Victorians were lavish in their use of this sweet hedgerow flower. Here are some ideas for using elderflowers to turn back the clock on some favourite Victorian dishes:

• Add one or two heads of the elderflower tied into muslin when making syrup for fruit salad, or when making gooseberry jelly, then discard the muslin bag.

• Strip the stalks and stir the flowers into a sweet pancake batter, or sponge sandwich mixture.

• Use elderflower syrup to make a sweetly refreshing sorbet (water ice), or add a muslin bag of the flowers when heating milk or cream to make ice cream.

• Pickle the small, pale green elderflower buds (stripped from the stalks) in vinegar and serve them as capers.

IT'S LEGENDARY

Legend had it that a child put to sleep in a cradle made of elder wood would be snatched by the fairies.

Elderflower 'champagne'

❖ Put the sugar, vinegar and water into a large earthenware crock or glass wine-making jar. Add the elderflowers, stripped of any leaves.

❖ Halve and squeeze the lemons and add the juice and pips. Slice the skins and add those too.

❖ Cover the crock or jar and set it aside for 48 hours, stirring it or shaking it occasionally.

❖ Strain the liquid into screw-topped or snap-top (ginger-beer type) bottles and leave them in a cool, dark place. The 'champagne' will be ready to drink within four or five days.

❖ Serve the drink chilled and decorated with borage flowers, lemon slices, scented geranium or mint leaves, or cucumber slices.

❖ Occasionally, for no apparent reason, the drink may lose some if its sparkle. Replace the tingle factor by mixing it half-and-half with fizzy lemonade or a dash of mineral water

Makes 5 litres (8 pints)

A PLATE POSY

Table Centrepieces

Victorian flower arrangers created ingenious adaptations of the familiar posy style. Miniature nosegays were placed at each setting around the table; lace-edged posies were set in tripod posy stands on side tables, and flat or pyramidal designs composed on footed stands or, more typically, glass or silver epergnes.

In a definitive manual of the time, *Fruit and Flower Decoration*, Mr T. C. March, a head gardener, set out the dos and don'ts of creating table centrepieces following the concentric ring principle. While many of his illustrations feature partnerships of lush ferns and contrasting foliage with a paucity of flowers, others show how to employ circles of a single flower type and a single colour to spectacular effect. Mr March considered yellow, purple and red to be compatible colours, and illustrated the point with three flat 'plate posies' side by side. Yellow, blue and pink was another approved combination, as was the even more restrained ring-a-ring arrangement of pink blossoms and small green leaves flanked on either side by all-white and foliage designs.

Restrained in the use of flowers, or exuberant with an abundance of blooms, the cascade posy shows the Victorian flair for floral art.

Arranging a plate posy

Since epergnes are somewhat difficult to come by, the design is created on a footed glass cake stand. A cylinder of absorbent stem-holding foam soaked in water serves as a moisture source for the foliage with long stems and feathery fronds. A shallow upturned basket helps to create the illusion of a cascade, and a slice of soaked foam on the basket holds short foliage sprays and flowers.

1 Arrange a ring of small evergreen leaves around the rim of the plate. Then build up the cascade of foliage, pushing the stems through the holes in the basket and into the foam.

2 Arrange separate leaves such as variegated periwinkle and scented geranium around the edge of the foam slice to form a continuous ring. The design is finished with a top-knot of heather and hellebores, Peruvian lilies (alstroemeria), freesias and spray chrysanthemums and decorated, in the manner of Victorian ferneries, with a silk butterfly.

VALENTINE TOKEN

A Lover's Chance

nder the supposed cloak of anonymity, Valentine cards gave shy Victorian lovers the chance to express feelings of admiration or adoration in terms that might not have tripped easily off the tongue. Flowery cards printed with sugar-sweet verses expressed or perhaps exaggerated the innermost thoughts and aspirations of would-be lovers, in much the same way that message posies did.

Verse writers of the time, calling upon the irresistible properties of flowers, spared no effort to bring about the perfect match. One Valentine card bearing the legend 'umbrella courtship' has this promise:

My heart is where true love reposes
I'll strew for you a bed of roses.

Another enticement, addressed to 'my pretty bird' puts the simple question, 'Will you come and dwell with me among the flowers?'

Flowers were pre-eminent, too, in the design of printed cards, with the meaningful language of flora a constant source of inspiration. Forget-me-nots and pansies, violets and roses, lilies-of-the-valley (signifying 'a return of happiness') and convolvulus (representing 'bonds') were popular floral images.

Valentine cards and pictures sent by sailors to the girl back home have long ago become collectors' items. One confident card, depicting Cupid, a bed of forget-me-nots and a lifebelt, bears the inscription 'I know a girl who's fond and true, and think that I deserve her. . .'

Hearts and flowers, ribbons and lace, satin and shells – Victorian Valentine tokens embraced them all. Our romantic interpretation of these declarations of love is typical of the time – a heart-shaped satin sleep pillow lined with unbleached calico and filled with rose petal and lavender pot pourri. The fresh flower posy carries its own message: red roses are for love, and white orchids for a belle. They were also thought to be aphrodisiacs.

A LOVE POSY

The Pursuit of Romance

earts and flowers brought together in the pursuit of romance are typified in this delightful love token – a small heart-shaped flower 'posy' that would convey its Valentine message from early morning until late in the evening, and beyond.

Place this delightfully fragrant decoration on a breakfast tray set with dainty Victorian china; tape it to the top of a ribboned gift box, or place it in the centre of a table set for dinner *à deux*. Carry it into the bedroom, where it will continue to convey its message and its aroma until the last minutes of Valentine's Day have ticked away.

YOU WILL NEED

* a block of absorbent stem-holding foam
* thick, self-adhesive parcel tape
* florists' fine silver wire
* a meaningful selection of flowers and foliage. Our choice was:
  white hyacinth, for unobtrusive loveliness
  blue hyacinth, for constancy
  pink hyacinth, for playfulness
  laurustinus, as a token
  ivy, for friendship, fidelity, marriage

1 Pick off the hyacinth florets and mount them on short pieces of silver wire. Twist the wire ends together to make false stems. Cut short lengths of all the other plant materials you have chosen for your love posy.

2 Cut a 2.5-cm (12-in) thick slice from the foam block, then cut out a heart shape. Cover the back with the parcel tape to prevent moisture from seeping through, then sprinkle the foam with water to soak it. Arrange the flowers to cover the heart on all sides.

SWEET NOTHINGS

Crystallized Flowers

Sugared violets and primroses, pansies and lilac florets, rosebuds and sweetly scented rose petals – Victorian ladies raised the use of these and other crystallized flowers to an art form. Carefully arranged into miniature posies or bouquets, scattered in profusion on iced gateaux and creamy desserts, used as a crowning glory a-top homemade chocolates, or packed between sheets of waxed paper and offered as enduring gifts – who could resist the symbolism of sweetly pretty flowers partially hiding their charms beneath a veil of powdered sugar?

Plucked from the garden and, if need be, dried on absorbent paper, the flowers, petals and leaves were painstakingly painted on all sides of every surface with a solution of gum arabic crystals and rosewater, to prevent air from reaching them, and sprinkled lightly with sugar. Nowadays, with gum arabic less readily available and its preparation seen as too time-consuming, lightly beaten egg white is more often used as the barrier coating.

To decorate heart-shaped Valentine cakes and other confections in this delightful way, select any edible flowers (see the panel on these pages) that have not been sprayed by harmful insecticides. Wash and dry them if necessary, gather together the few ingredients you need, and settle down to start a therapeutic task that is rich in Victorian nostalgia.

YOU WILL NEED

+ selection of edible flowers, petals or leaves
+ egg white
+ caster sugar
+ small, bristle paint brush

1 Lightly beat the egg white in a small bowl. Holding the petals or other plant materials with tweezers, or by their stems, paint them on all sides with the egg white.

Two heart-shaped Valentine cakes covered in soft pink fondant icing are decorated with crystallized rose petals, rosebuds and pineapple mint, and with a posy of sugared pansies and violet leaves.

2 Sprinkle the petals lightly with sugar and shake them gently to remove any excess. Too much sugar will completely mask the flowers' characteristic charms. Spread the sugared flowers on a wire rack and leave them in a warm, dry place such as an airing cupboard for several hours. Store them between sheets of kitchen paper in airtight tins or boxes.

EDIBLE FLOWERS

Check that any flowers you pick are edible before you use them to decorate food. These are a few of the prettiest:

ALMOND BLOSSOM	FORGET-ME-NOT	ORANGE BLOSSOM
APPLE BLOSSOM	HONEYSUCKLE	PANSY
BROOM	JASMINE	PRIMROSE
CARNATION	LAVENDER	ROSE
CLOVER	LILAC	SWEET WILLIAM
DAISY	MIMOSA	VIOLET
ELDERFLOWER	NASTURTIUM	

PANSIES, THAT'S FOR THOUGHTS

Pillow Talk

A romantic gift prettily wrapped in ribbons and lace and placed, secretly, on a pillow is designed to speak volumes. When the parcel wrapping is decorated with a nosegay of pansies and rosemary, tiny violas and ivy trails, the hidden message becomes more meaningful still.

Ever since Shakespeare's day and perhaps long before, pansies have signified thoughts. It was Ophelia in *Hamlet* who said,

> *There's rosemary, that's for remembrance;*
> *Pray love remember; and there is pansies –*
> *That's for thoughts.*

These symbolic meanings were given new currency in several Victorian dictionaries of flower names, the language of flora, where we find that violas can be shown to mean, 'You are queen of my coquettes,' and are reminded that ivy, the plant that was sacred to Bacchus, god of wine, was the symbol of faithfulness.

Decorating the parcel

The gift box is wrapped in crisp, lightly starched white cotton secured with neat stitches. (Double-sided sticky tape would be less traditional, but equally effective.)

The parcel is then covered on each side with a lace-edged and loosely woven place mat; the kind of Victorian treasure you might find in a shop specializing in linens.

The posy is composed in the hand, the flowers placed at graduated levels so that each pansy face is seen to full advantage. The stems are bound with white twine and left in water until it is time to sew them onto the gift and place it on the pillow.

JUST DREAMY

When the Victorians drew a connection between pansies and pillow talk, they were simply following Oberon's lead. In *A Midsummer Night's Dream* he despatches Puck to find for him

> *. . . love-in-idleness.*
> *The juice of it on sleeping eyelids laid*
> *Will make man or women madly dote*
> *Upon the next live creature that it sees.*

PANSY JELLY

Thoughtful Hostesses

As pansies are for thoughts (their name is derived from the French word *pensée*, a thought), thoughtful Victorian hostesses served light and refreshing pansy jelly as a lunchtime dessert, or as an interlude between the main course and a rich pudding. Set in fine claret glasses or decorative moulds, each jelly enclosed a perfect specimen flower, its 'three-faces-under-a-hood' upturned for the prettiest effect. Tiny meringues or *langues du chat* biscuits were usually served with the dessert.

Decorative pottery and copper moulds were a feature of Victorian kitchens and used extensively for shaping jellies, creams and mousses.

Champagne jelly with pansies

⟿ SERVES 4 ⟾

Sparkling white wine or, best of all, Champagne, makes this a dessert to remember.

YOU WILL NEED

❖ 2 sachets of gelatin crystals, about 30 g (1 oz) each
❖ 45 ml (3 tbsp) water
❖ thinly pared zest and juice of 2 lemons
❖ 100 g (4 oz) sugar
❖ 1 stick cinnamon
❖ whites and finely crushed shells of 2 eggs
❖ 150 ml (5 fl oz) Champagne, or other sparkling white wine
❖ 4 pansy flowers, washed and dried

❖ Dissolve the gelatin crystals in the water. Put the lemon zest, lemon juice, sugar and cinnamon into an enamel pan. Pour on 450 ml (16 fl oz) of water and stir over medium heat until the sugar dissolves. Remove the pan from the heat, discard the cinnamon and stir in the dissolved gelatin.

❖ Beat the egg whites and shells until they are frothy. Pour them into the pan, add the wine until the mixture reaches simmering point.

❖ Remove the pan from the heat and set it aside until the froth subsides.

❖ Reheat and set aside the mixture twice more, then finally leave it to cool.

❖ Line a sieve with a double thickness of scalded muslin. Place the sieve over a jug and pour in the jelly to extract the eggshell.

❖ Divide the jelly between four glasses, reserving a little to cover the pansies, and place in a refrigerator. When set, place a pansy in each glass, melt the reserved jelly and pour over the pansies. Leave until the top is set.

❖ To set the jelly in a mould, rinse it in cold water, pour in a little of the jelly to cover the base and place one or more pansies face down on top of the jelly. Gently push the pansies into the jelly and leave them to set. Pour on the remaining jelly to fill the mould, and set it in the refrigerator.

❖ Run a knife round the inside of the mould and invert it onto a serving plate. Decorate with fresh pansies.

A romantic ring of pressed pansies.

PANSY RING

Sweet, Smiling Faces

Press the sweet, almost smiling faces of blue, yellow and purple pansies and you capture their beauty, and their romantic meaning for generations to come.

Victorian children loved to press them and arrange them, identifying perhaps with their innocent appeal. Lovers loved to find one or two pressed flowers enclosed between the pages of a favourite book. And Victorian ladies took them to their hearts, composing pressed pansy flowers into bouquets and rings, and pasting them onto birthday cards to signify their loving thoughts.

AFFECTIONATE NICKNAMES

The Victorians' fondness for nicknames found free and amusing expression in the pretty names by which pansies were known. The ancient name of *banewort* was dropped in favour of *herb constancy* and *herb trinitatis*, and other country names are *call-me-to-you*, *heart's ease*, *Jack-jump-up-and-kiss-me*, *Kit-run-in-the-fields*, *little-my-fancy*, *love-in-idleness*, *loving-thoughts*, *pink-of-my-John*, *stepfathers and stepmothers*, and *three-faces-under-a-hood*.

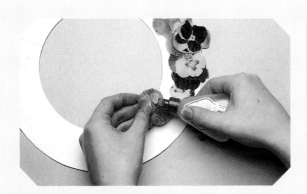

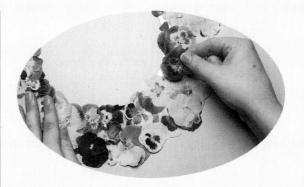

1 To make the pressed pansy ring, cut a circle of stiff card about 25 cm (10 in) in diameter and with a depth of about 7.5 cm (2½ in). Use clear papercraft glue to stick on a ring of pansies around one rim, overlapping the flowers to cover the card completely.

2 Save the prettiest pansies and those in the strongest colours until last. When the ring is covered, press it between large sheets of white paper under a heavy weight. The ring looks pretty under the glass top of a dressing table or coffee table, or in an old maple frame.

FLOWER DECORATED EGGS

Eastertime Traditions

Victorian families developed an enchanting variety of individual traditions at Eastertime. In some households the children spent many happy hours during Lent decorating eggshells with floral découpage scraps or pictures cut from magazines, dyeing hard-boiled eggs or blown eggshells with plant dyes (onion skins for a deep, rich brown were a favourite), painting eggs with spots, stars, stripes or floral motifs, or covering them with a natural collage of pressed flowers such as buttercups or daisies.

In other families, the parents, older children and aunts decorated the eggs, then concealed them in nooks and crannies around the house and, in fine weather, in the garden, and the younger children raced off to hunt for them. Some eggs might be artistically decorated with pressed flowers and varnished to look like hand-painted china. Others were covered with a rich tapestry of dressmaking scraps – embroidered ribbon, braid, buttons and beads – and fashioned to look like the priceless eggs created by the Russian artist Fabergé. Painted or dyed, floral or beribboned, however they were decorated, to the children who found them the eggs represented the priceless treasure of Eastertime.

In this delightful tradition, eggs decorated with pressed flowers can become precious family possessions, even heirlooms. Blown and decorated eggs may be hung on ribbons from a vase of twigs that are about to burst into bud at Eastertime, or carefully saved until Christmas when, after the fashion set by Queen Victoria's husband, Prince Albert, they may be hung like glistening baubles on the Christmas tree.

The egg yolks and whites blown from their shells become the ingredients for Easter cakes, biscuits, ice creams and puddings. And if the eggshells are small enough – such as those of bantam's eggs – they can be clustered in a sugar-paste nest and assembled in the place of honour, on top of the Easter cake.

To blow eggshells

Use a darning needle to pierce a hole in each end of the egg and stir it around inside to break the yolk. Then, holding the egg over a bowl, blow through one of the holes. The contents should flow out in a steady stream.

To decorate the eggs

You can paint empty eggshells with watercolour or acrylic paints, spray them with non-toxic paint from a can or immerse them in purple and red fruit juices from mulberries, blackberries, raspberries and blackcurrants. Alternatively, boil eggs in fruit juices or food colouring for about an hour, and the eggs should be well preserved.

❖ Sort through your collection of pressed flowers, petals and leaves and select the smallest and least substantial ones. Large, thick specimens will not easily take up the contours of the eggshell; and the more flimsy the flowers, the more ethereal and pretty the effect will be.

A long-abandoned bird's nest filled with painted and flower-decorated eggs makes an appropriate table decoration for Easter morning.

❖ Spread a thin layer of papercraft glue over the whole surface of the eggshell, or on the area to be decorated. Press the plant materials in place and stand the eggs on little stilts to dry. A row of dressmakers' pins stuck into a block of florists' foam makes an ideal support system.

❖ When the glue has dried, paint or spray the eggs with varnish and leave them to dry again. For a découpage look, build up several coats of varnish, leaving the eggs to dry between each one.

FLOWERS FOR CHURCH

Eastertime Expression

The Victorian lady's enthusiasm for arranging flowers found full expression at Eastertime, which was the first main religious festival of the year. Those who volunteered to arrange flowers in the church planned their designs months in advance, making sure that their glasshouses would be able to offer rich pickings of colourful blooms, and that there would be enough garden flowers to make their Easter displays as delightful as possible.

The designs they created in church displayed the same fondness for deep, rich, warm tones that characterized floral displays in the home and were used with comparable abundance. Wooden laths were bent and covered with greenery to form verdant arches. Baskets of flowers stood on windowsills and at the base of lecterns and pulpits; pyramid-shaped arrangements graced hymn-book tables, pedestal stands and piano tops; and swags were hung from the ends of pews, in niches and on screens.

Composing a vertical swag

A large ribbon bow at the top of the decoration and a pair of trailing ribbons beneath it create the illusion that the swag is composed on a ribbon strip. Pale lavender ribbon and pale and deep mauve freesias are the keynotes of the decoration, both appropriate to the celebration of the Easter festival, and favourites of the Victorian lady. We chose paper ribbon, or you could use silk or satin ribbons for a more opulent appearance.

YOU WILL NEED

* absorbent stem-holding foam, soaked in water
* knife
* filmwrap
* florists' scissors
* florists' tape (optional)
* plastic foam holders (optional)
* medium-gauge stub wires
* paper ribbon
* slender foliage trails such as weeping willow or small-leaved ivy
* selection of flowers such as laurustinus and freesias

1 Either cut one rectangular block of soaked foam and wrap it in filmwrap, or cut two smaller blocks and wrap them and tape them into plastic foam-holding 'cages'. Cut two lengths of ribbon for the trails and another for the bow, and fix them into the foam with twisted stub wires. Arrange long foliage trails to extend beneath the decoration and shorter ones slanted outwards at varying angles throughout the design.

2 Cut short stems of laurustinus and arrange them along the length of the foam, so that they partially conceal it. Fill in the design with freesias, the pale and deep tones arranged alternately. Spray the flowers with cool water and, if possible, position the decoration away from strong sunlight.

An Easter symbol

Floral crosses closely studded with primroses, violets and lilies-of-the-valley were made for Victorian children to carry in Easter processions. These floral crosses were also placed around the church font as special decorations during this religious festival.

The one shown here is made of three narrow blocks of floral foam that were soaked in water and then wrapped in filmwrap. The foam was threaded onto split canes bound into the shape of a cross. You need to pierce holes in the filmwrap with a skewer so that the delicate stems can reach the moisture source.

Rhapsody in blue

The child's bonnet in the photograph is fitted with a wire band closely bound with pink braid and then, loosely and casually, with pink and white gingham ribbon tied in a simple bow at the back. Small posies of forget-me-nots and daisy-like spray chrysanthemum buds are bound onto the band to form a continuous line half-way around the crown. Just one scarlet dwarf tulip is included for contrast, and to appeal to a young child's love of all things bright and beautiful.

EASTER BONNETS

Decked with Flowers

Flowers have always gone straight to little girls' heads. Generations of young ladies must have danced up and down with excitement at the prospect of wearing flower-decked bonnets just like Mama's on Easter morning and enthusiastically played their part in designing the floral decorations.

In Victorian times, when intricate straw plaiting was such a labour-intensive cottage industry in country districts, panama hats and other straw hats descriptively referred to as 'pudding basin styles' were popular with mothers and daughters alike. The golden plaited straw, with just a hint of sunshine sparkle, was the perfect material to set off dainty posies or headband-garlands of garden or countryside flowers; the hats and their floral decorations seemed to be made for each other.

Children's Easter bonnets look prettiest when they are adorned with flowers that little girls have always loved to pick – forget-me-nots and pansies, buttercups and daisies, ragged robin (campion) and hedgerow roses. Although the temptation must always be to turn a handful of flowers into an instant millinery masterpiece, children should be encouraged to put flowers in water first, to give them the best chance of lasting the course without fading or wilting.

CHILDHOOD DELIGHT

Buttercups and Daisies

Generations of young children have scampered like puppies through fields of buttercups, sunk down in mock exhaustion and picked one of the golden round-faced flowers to hold under a companion's chin. The answer to the question, 'Do you like butter?' was an unqualified 'yes' if the bright buttery-yellow flower was reflected on the other child's skin.

Generations of children, too, have giggled with delight at the perceived naughtiness of the accompanying rhyme,

> *Do you like butter?*
> *Do you like tea?*
> *Do you like sitting on your sweetheart's knee?*

Not surprisingly, in the Victorian language of flowers buttercups signified childishness, innocence and fidelity. The ways that children then and now enjoy these meadow flowers, which verge on weeds, are faithful to that tradition.

Children love to pick a handful of the flowers as a present for Mama, to 'arrange' them in a used preserve jar, or to tie them for a homeward journey with a few supple stalks of grass. And the bright, shiny irresistible flowers have introduced many children to the art of flower pressing. Weeks later, when rows of flowers are at last ready to be uncovered, children have been delighted to discover that they have lost none of their colour or characteristic gloss – and certainly none of their charm.

Buttercup and daisy drink

SERVES 4

This refreshing and thirst-quenching drink is adapted from a Victorian summertime favourite, so named because of its yellow and white colouring.

YOU WILL NEED

- ❖ 600 ml (1 pint) plain yoghurt
- ❖ 300 ml (½ pint) lime cordial
- ❖ 300 ml (½ pint) sparkling mineral water
- ❖ ice cubes or crushed ice
- ❖ slices of lime or lemon
- ❖ mint sprigs, variegated if available

❖ Chill the yoghurt, lime cordial and mineral water. Whisk them together or process them in a blender until they are frothy. Pour the drink over ice and decorate each glass with lime or lemon slices and mint sprigs. Serve chilled.

THE SWEETEST PLEASURE

Daisy Chains

Not until you can put your foot on seven daisies, runs the proverb, has summer come. But weeks before that time arrived, sometimes as early as March, it was one of spring's sweetest pleasures for a little girl to make a daisy chain to hang around her wrist or ankle, to wear like a crown on her head, or hang around her doll's neck.

Children seemed to know by instinct how to make these continuous flower chains, using a finger nail to make a slit in one daisy stem, pushing another through it, slitting that one, and so on, until the chain was long enough for its proud intended purpose.

Small posies of some all-white, some pink-tinged daisies – surely among the most enchanting of flower clusters – would be bound onto circlets of grass stems. These more substantial daisy rings were worn as floral headdresses or carried as hoops at weddings and springtime festivals. They also make delightfully simple short-term wall or table decorations, pretty reminders of childhood past.

Making a daisy chain

Slit one stem and push another one through. Slit that stem and so on, until the daisy chain is long enough.

EYE-OPENER

It is thought that the daisy (Latin name *Bellis perennis*) got its name because it opens its petals during daylight and closes them at night; one of the popular names for the flowers is day's eye.

Other country names for the tiny composite flowers are *bachelor's buttons, bairnwort, bennergowan, bennest, bessy-banwood, billy button, boneflower, catposy, cockilo-orie, cumfirie, daiseyghe, dazey, disk daisy, dog daisy, hen and chickens, herb Margaret, little Easter flower, march daisy, Margaret's herb, marguerite, Mary Gowlan, maudlinwort, measure of love, mother of thousands, silver penny, sweep,* and *thousand charms.*

A buttercup and daisy ring

Supple grass stems are bound with twine to make a simple circlet. Then small bunches of fresh daisies and unruly bunches of buttercups are bound in random order around the grass ring.

It is advisable to give the flowers a good long drink of water before arranging them.

SWEET VIOLETS

A Victorian Delicacy

CRYSTALLIZED VIOLETS

Crystallized violets decorating desserts and bon-bons, a glass of violet wine to while away a summer's afternoon, violet tea, syrup, jam, jelly, vinegar, butter – Victorian ladies explored every culinary avenue to capture the sweet scent of the violet flower and translate it into delicacies of all kinds.

Violet tea

The Duchess of Kent, Queen Victoria's mother, favoured violet tea that was made, like other tisanes, by steeping 5 ml (1 tsp) of dried violets in a cup of boiling water for five or ten minutes. Unlike some other tisanes, this one did not need sweetening with honey.

Violet syrup

Queen Victoria preferred to enjoy the sweet fragrance of violets in the form of a syrup. This was made to a recipe calling for 225 g (8 oz) of dried violet flowers, twice that amount of powdered sugar, 25 g (1 oz) gum arabic crystals, 5 g (1 tsp) dried orris-root powder and 250 ml (8 fl oz) boiling water. When the syrup was cooled and bottled, it could be diluted to drink as a soothing cordial, used in desserts or as a pouring sauce over ice cream.

A tiny nosegay of crystallized violets and African violets (Saintpaulia) makes an enchanting table decoration.

Violet mousse

Violet mousse was a favourite dessert of the time, made by flavouring the dairy-rich confection of eggs, cream, gelatin and sugar with violet extract or violet syrup. The top of the mousse would be decorated with a flamboyant display of crystallized violets, the flowers and their leaves arranged in concentric rings in the style of a circular posy, or made up into dainty and delicate nosegays. Sometimes these nosegays were offered as a sugary token to each lady around the table, the preserved flowers placed on a folded napkin or a small salad plate, with a take-home box thoughtfully provided. The method for crystallizing violets and other flowers is given on pages 26 and 27.

Violet wine

Dainty bouquets of stemmed violets are one thing, Victorian-style violet wine another. By present-day standards the Victorians made extravagant use of flowers in the preparation of their wines and liqueurs. A recipe instructing the reader to 'take one gallon [5 litres] of violet petals' would find little favour now. It is possible, though, to savour the fragrance and the flavour of the flowers by steeping them in an inexpensive medium-dry white wine.

To do this, tie 15 ml (1 tbsp) violet flowers in a piece of scalded muslin and immerse them in a bottle of wine

Violet wine and chocolates decorated with crystallized violet flowers, two ways in which the Victorians captured the delicate fragrance of the flowers.

for seven days. Repeat the process with fresh flowers, then taste the wine. If you want to strengthen the violet flavour still further, repeat the process once more. Remove the flowers and, if any stray petals have escaped, strain the wine through clean muslin. Serve the wine lightly chilled, as a 'social drink'. It was customary to offer it in mid-morning with a slice of Madeira cake, or in the afternoon with a selection of iced fancies.

A PLANTED BASKET

Twigs, Primroses and Violets

here is nostalgia in the style of this basket, made of rough twigs nailed to a wooden frame and planted with violets. Baskets like this, though larger, were carried from door to door by gypsy girls selling springtime posies of primroses and violets. And there is Victorian authenticity, too, in the notion of combining flowering plants with cut flowers in water, or foliage plants with a hidden vase as a moisture source for showy blooms. Today's *pot et fleur* combinations of growing plants and gathered flowers have design origins that date back to the early Victorian era.

To plant a basket of this kind, line it with dry moss, and then with a polythene sheet. Set one or more African violet or sweet violet plants in potting compost on one side, and surround a small water-holding container with more compost on the other. Gather a small bunch of primroses or other tiny spring flowers, including a few leaves, and put them in water. Cover the peat and surround the flowers with a few tufts of fresh green moss.

SNIPPETS FROM FRANCE

There are strong connections between the Emperor Napoleon and that most delicate of flowers, the sweet violet. Napoleon was often referred to as '*Papa la Violette*' or '*Caporal la Violette*', a reference to the assumption that he would return to Elba in the spring. When he did so, his way was strewn with violets. Ladies who gathered to receive him wore violet-coloured gowns and carried posies of the Emperor's favourite flowers, which they showered on him when he entered the palace. And when Eugenie became Empress of France, her wedding garland was composed of sweet violets encircled with their leaves.

Lord Byron has Napoleon, on his departure for Elba, dramatically declaring:

Farewell to thee, France! but when liberty rallies
Once more in thy regions, remember me then,
The Violet grows in the depth of thy valleys,
Though withered, thy tears will unfold it again.

MAYTIME FESTIVALS

Floral Wreath

The flowers that bloom in the spring have always encouraged people to lift up their hearts. In ancient times, the reassuring signs of new growth in the countryside were celebrated with the festival of flora, when homes and places of worship, celebrants and even the trees were garlanded with flowers, and walls and doors were hung with floral rings.

This custom of expressing joy in the springtime flowers lived on through the Victorian age, when Mayday festivals were held on village greens, and houses in some country regions were decked out with floral wreaths and garlands as a signal that at last winter had passed. The festival of May, *protomayia*, is still marked in this way in Greece where a floral ring, known as a *stefani*, is hung on front doors as a sign of good luck and welcome.

A floral ring

The floral ring shown here captures the spirit of carefree Victorian festivals, when doors and windows were opened wide, every visitor was a friend and a loving cup of homemade wine was passed from hand to hand.

Leave the flowers in water for as long as possible. As it takes only a few minutes to compose the wreath, it is best to leave its construction until the last minute.

> ### YOU WILL NEED
>
> ❖ a wreath base, bought from a florist or made from supple stems
> ❖ a selection of springtime flowers, as varied and as colourful as possible
> ❖ florists' fine silver wire
> ❖ green garden twine

1 Compose some of the smaller flowers into bunches and bind the stems with silver wire. Bind bunches and single stems alternately around the ring, pulling the twine tightly at each turn.

2 Continue until the ring is covered with flowers, and fasten off the twine. Spray the ring with cool water and, if possible, hang it where it will not be in the full glare of the sun.

FLORAL HEAD-DRESS
Headbands and Garlands

oung Victorian girls loved to wear flowers in their hair. Small posies tied with ribbons would be tucked into Sunday-best hair-styles; headbands covered with fresh or dried flowers were fashionable headgear for parties; and floral garlands or crowns were worn on highdays and holidays, at spring and summer festivals, and by bridesmaids and young brides on their wedding day.

Countryside flowers have a more youthful appeal than formal blooms cultivated in glasshouses. But these flowers tend to be more vulnerable and to suffer more from the lack of a moisture source, so they need to be put into water as soon as they are gathered, and left there until the last possible moment.

A head-dress composed of mixed nosegays bound onto a wire band meets these criteria. You can make it from mixed bunches of flowers and light foliage bound into small posies and left in cool water in a cool place until minutes before the event. It is a matter of only moments to bind them onto a circlet.

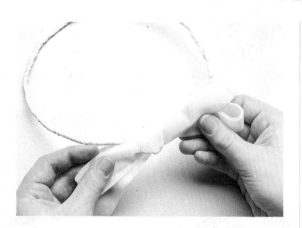

1 Measure a length of flexible wire that will fit comfortably on the head. Overlap the ends and bind them together with fine silver wire. Bind the circlet with ribbon, then bind on a ribbon bow, leaving trailing ends if you wish. Velvet was popular with the Victorians.

2 Make up posies of small spring flowers such as lords and ladies (pulmonaria), primroses, jonquils and mimosa, and variegated geranium leaves. When you are ready to compose the garland, bind on the posies so that the tips of each one cover the stems of the one before.

A floral head-dress fit for a fairy princess.

PROCESSION POSIES

For Weddings and Festivals

ittle girls in starched white dresses and little boys in velvet knickers and goffered shirts, generations of young children have carried pyramidal posies at weddings and springtime festivals, some with all the solemnity of dignitaries carrying a mace or a staff on more austere occasions.

The practice of mounting posies on bamboo canes, so that they could be carried aloft and more readily admired, was especially associated with Mayday celebrations. Similar compositions of flowers were used to decorate maypoles around which the children danced, weaving their way over and under the coloured ribbons fixed to the top of the pole.

With the dignity of young boys in mind, we chose a blue and yellow colour theme for the flowers, and decorated the pole with long trails of toning blue and cream embroidered ribbons tied in a double bow.

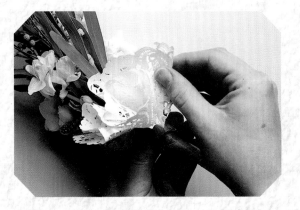

1 Bind a bamboo cane with ribbon and fasten the ends. Cut flower stems to short, even lengths and leave them in water for as long as possible. Bind the first few stems of mimosa to the top of the pole, then surround it with another circle of flowers such as double white jonquils.

2 Bind on another circle of flowers, such as grape hyacinths, with their heads at a lower level, then bind the stems securely. Cut a hole in the centre of two paper doilies, push the pole through, and bind the 'frill' in place. Tie trailing ribbons around the pole.

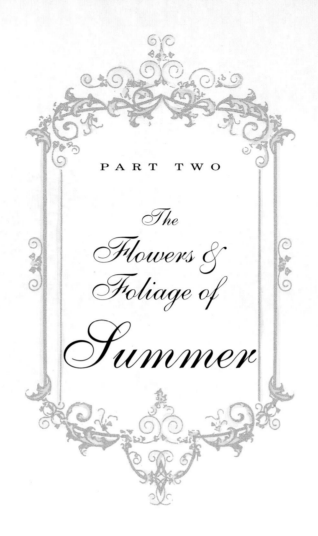

PART TWO

The

Flowers &

Foliage of

Summer

Baskets filled with lavender, and paths scattered with

rose petals. Tussie-mussies (little nosegays) of fragrant herbs plucked from

the garden, and a secret tryst between lovers in a flower-filled meadow.

The romance of a traditional posy of rosebuds and orange blossom, and the

celebration of a wedding in the family. These are the evocative memories

of a Victorian lady's summer that linger in these pages.

LAVENDER BLUE

The Essence of Summer

 shallow trug basket of blue-purple lavender – the essence of summer.

It is a decoration which brings to mind billowing fields carpeted in mid-summer with this heady-scented plant which, the Victorians said, 'breathes of Paradise'. It evokes the lingering and mingled scents of a herb garden on a summer's eve, when just to brush against a lavender bush is to experience a tremor of excitement. It recalls country-house drawing-rooms where bowls of the minute flowers were there for guests to stir, in passing, with their fingers to release the fragrance anew. And it evokes cleanliness and health, comfort and relaxation.

The decoration is reminiscent, too, of the lavender sellers who cried their wares through the streets of Victorian England, with this sing-song refrain,

Lavender, sweet blooming Lavender,
Six bunches a penny to-day.
Lavender, sweet blooming Lavender
Ladies buy it while you may.

The plant's name is derived from the Latin *lavare*, to wash, since the Romans liked to bathe in the lavender-scented water. Little changed through the ages. Who does not have images of Victorian ladies taking comfort from lavender-scented handkerchiefs, or coyly dropping a hankie at the feet of their beaux?

The flower's meaning is acknowledgement, and when it is made into bunches it signifies industry.

Our shallow trug basket is lined with lightly starched cotton and lace tray cloths and filled, industriously, with small bunches of lavender, the stems of each one bound with colourless thread. Arranged at random among the lavender flowers, and adding to the ode-to-a-summer's-day intention, there are clusters of dried red roses; just for love.

A note of thrift

Be like thrifty Victorian housewives and gather up all the lavender flowers that fall as you tie the bunches. They have their place in the sachets on the following pages.

*A basket of lavender and old lace
evokes the aura of Victorian summers.*

SCENTING THE AIR

Lavender Bags

From the bedroom to the drawing-room, the linen cupboard to the clothes closet, the scent of lavender filled the air. 'Sweet bags' of lavender flowers were hung from the bedposts and tucked under pillows, hung from the backs of chairs and tucked beneath antimacassars and chair-back covers. No pile of freshly laundered linen was put away without its complement of muslin or linen lavender sachets concealed beneath the layers of bedsheets and pillowcases, bath towels and tablecloths; and no gowns or undergarments were thought sweet-smelling and fresh enough to be worn unless they, too, had been impregnated with the clean, fresh scent of lavender.

Dried lavender flowers, retaining the most pervasive of all floral scents, were often used alone to fill sachets and dolly bags, tiny pillows and even frivolous garters. They were also used as the principal ingredients in 'sweet mixtures', when they were blended with other dried flowers and petals to compose a medley of floral scents. A typical recipe, including dried orris-root powder as a fixative, is given opposite.

The skill of blending floral fragrances and the gentle art of needlework came together with delightful results in the creation of lavender bags and sweet bags, and where their design was concerned, ingenuity knew no bounds. Small rectangular bags were made from scraps of furnishing or fashion material, be it silk or satin, cotton or linen, and tied close to the top with fancy ribbons. Decorative ribbon was used in a similar way to make bags for the sweet mixtures.

Lengths of wide satin ribbon were folded, hemmed along the sides and across the top and tied with narrow and contrasting ribbons to secure the contents but allow the fragrance to be released.

Circular placemats, dressing-table mats and cotton doilies were used in two different ways, to make small dolly bags or sweet pillows. If you can find lace-edged Victorian placemats in the 'linen box' section of an antique shop or a street market, both ideas promise decorative results and instant nostalgia.

The dolly bags are made by piling a spoonful of dried lavender flowers or sweet mixture in the centre of a cotton or linen mat, drawing up the sides and tying around with ribbon. The lacier the placemat, the better.

To make small pillows, select two placemats, place them together, right sides inwards, and sew around the panels. Leave a small hole for filling. Turn the placemats inside-out, fill with flowers and sew up the opening.

To make a flower-scented garter, cut wide elastic to fit around the thigh, cut two lengths of ribbon, each twice that length, sew them together, and thread the elastic through. Sew up one end and spoon in your flowers from the other. Sew the ends together to secure the elastic.

Sweet-bag mixture

Mix all the ingredients together and store in a lidded container for one week, stirring daily before using to fill bags and sachets.

PURE ROMANCE

Peony and Lavender Wreath

he scent of lavender; the voluptuous appeal of sugar almond-pink peony flowers; the romance of rosebuds, and the snowy-whiteness of crisply starched cotton, all come together in a nostalgic decoration with a high tingle factor and a special scent.

The peony and lavender wreath, which has all the glamour associated with a Victorian bedroom, would look enchanting hanging on a wall or wardrobe door, placed on a bedside table or hanging on a bedpost. Its lingering aroma and pretty colour contrasts are irresistibly romantic.

To make the wreath

1 Arrange the lavender bunches in clusters, facing in opposite directions and leaving spaces for the peonies and the lace decoration. Attach the bunches to the ring with glue, or with U-shaped staples made by bending halved stub wires. Glue peony flowers in place, and ease out the petals to give them a three-dimensional look. Then glue a rosebud in the centre of each peony.

YOU WILL NEED

❖ vine wreath, 25cm (10in) in diameter
❖ lace-edged cotton place mat, about 25cm (10in) in diameter
❖ small bunches of dried lavender
❖ dried peonies
❖ dried rosebuds
❖ 2.5-cm(1in)-wide pleated or shirred ribbon
❖ florists' fine silver wire
❖ florists' scissors
❖ medium-gauge stub wires
❖ wire cutters
❖ hot glue gun, or clear, quick-setting glue

$\mathscr{2}$ Make accordian pleats across the place mat and tie it in the centre with the decorative ribbon. Attach the 'bow' to the base of the ring with glue or with a wire taken through the back of the ribbon loop. Ease out the lace to make a bow shape, and neaten the ends of the ribbon.

A LOVER'S TRYST

Two's Company

It is a balmy summer afternoon. The doves are cooing, the bees humming, and there is not a cloud in the sky. Two young lovers, Sarah and William, set off from opposite sides of the village to meet for a secret picnic by the brook.

Hidden somewhere among the provisions is a posy that the young man has composed in the Victorian tradition for his sweetheart. It does not have nor does it need ribbons and lace. Its meaning is clear. At the centre is a deep red rosebud as a declaration of his true love. As if that were not enough, he has added clove gillyflowers (pinks) to signify bonds of affection, and marigolds, which in the language of flowers represent a prediction: this time, perhaps, her answer will be yes?

Small sprays of early Michaelmas daisies, a note of contrasting colour among the warm red and flame tones, were included as an afterthought, which is their symbolic meaning.

The young girl chooses a single flower species to signify her admiration and trust in her beau. She decorates her new hat with a band of magenta velvet ribbon and a circlet of flowers dedicated to sweet William. Their symbolic meaning, and perhaps one of his endearing characteristics, is gallantry.

To decorate the hat

Sarah's hat, with a shallow crown and wide brim, is woven of rushes. To decorate a similar hat with a circlet of fresh flowers, cut a ribbon band to fit exactly around the brim of the hat, making a small allowance for turnings. Tie a flat bow from matching ribbon and sew it to one end of the band.

Make your selection of flowers and put them in water for several hours, or overnight. Cut the stems short, dry them and sew them to the hatband; then tack the band in place with a few large stitches.

Everlasting flowers, symbols of everlasting love, make a pretty and long-lasting hat decoration. Tack or stick a narrow ribbon band around the brim, then stick dried strawflowers, helipterum (rhodanthe), poppy seedheads and miniature sprays of baby's breath (gypsophilia) around it. A generous bow of cream lace ribbon trim gives the hat a truly Victorian flourish.

A PRESSING ENGAGEMENT

Romantic Mementoes

An anniversary card made up of a bouquet of pressed leaves and flowers; a few sprays of flowers newly discovered between the pages of an old book; a pressed flower sampler hanging over a bed-head, the flowers, leaflets and petals spelling out two names or representing two initials entwined – what nostalgic memories these one-dimensional flowers can stir.

The Victorians, who developed flower-pressing to state-of-the-art craftsmanship, liked to press flowers where they grew. In this way, they captured the plant material in peak condition, before it had time to wilt on a long homeward journey. And they laid in store romantic mementoes of happy occasions – a meadowside picnic enjoyed by two young lovers, a first date, a proposal of marriage, or a honeymoon idyll.

For such a romantic notion to have such pleasing results, a little forethought is called for. Not everyone setting out to spend a lazy afternoon in the sun just happens to be carrying a heavy book or a flower press, some sheets of absorbent paper, a small pair of scissors, tweezers and a small paint brush.

The last three items are optional extras, which might be thought to rob the desire to press flowers 'on site' of any degree of spontaneity. But they do make it easier to snip off stems neatly and arrange the plant material.

Pressing flowers

1 Arrange flowers, leaves or sprays of roughly equal thickness on each sheet of absorbent paper, and position them so that no two are touching. Those shown here are buttercups and campion.

Preserved in an old wooden flower press, buttercups and sweet William flowers will keep alive happy memories of a summer picnic.

2 Carefully lower the second sheet of paper on top, without creating a rush of air that would disarrange the flowers.

3 Put the sheets of absorbent paper under heavy pressure. If the plant material is thick and has a great deal of residual moisture, replace the absorbent paper every day for the next two or three days. Then leave the flower press or book in a dry place for several weeks until the materials are perfectly preserved.

FROM THE ROSE GARDEN

Teatime with Roses

The heady scent of roses was one of the most enduring of the Victorian era. The sometimes spicy, sometimes sweet and always alluring blend of fragrances that wafted from the rose garden became more than a lovely lingering memory as imaginative cooks 'put up' rose-scented preserves and confections.

Rose-petal jam to serve on toasted teacakes or, a delicious combination, on cinnamon toast; rose-petal jelly (there is a recipe on pages 128 and 129) to serve with light-as-air scones and clotted cream; sponge sandwich cake lightly scented with rosewater; and cherry and rose-petal 'cheese' to set in moulds and serve with sliced teabread – in these and many other ways the scent of roses lingered from one flowering season to the next.

Choose the most fragrant rose petals you have. Discard any damaged ones, pick off the creamy-white part at the base of each petal and, if the bushes have been sprayed with an insecticide or are close to a road, wash and dry the petals carefully, without bruising them.

Rose-petal jam

Use the preserve sparingly, on toast or as a filling for sponge sandwich cakes.

YOU WILL NEED

- 2 cups scented rose petals
- 675 g (1½ lb) sugar
- 2 large cooking apples, peeled, cored and chopped
- 300 ml (½ pint) water
- 30 ml (2 tbsp) lemon juice

❖ Tear the rose petals into small pieces and place them in a non-metal bowl. Pour on half the sugar, cover the bowl and set it aside for two days.

❖ Put the remaining sugar, the apples, water and lemon juice in a pan and stir over low heat until the sugar has dissolved. Simmer, stirring occasionally, until the apples have collapsed. Add the rose petals and sugar and stir well.

❖ Bring to the boil and fast-boil for 20 minutes, or until a little of the preserve spooned onto a cold saucer will set.

❖ Pour the preserve into small, warm sterilized jars, cover the surface with waxed discs and cover the jars with jam-pot covers or screw-on lids. Label the jars and store them in a cool, dark place.

Makes about 1 kg (2¼ lb) preserve

Cherry and rose-petal 'cheese'

This rich, glowing preserve may also be served with cold ham, poultry and game.

YOU WILL NEED

- 450 g (1 lb) cherries
- 1 cup scented rose petals
- 90 ml (6 tbsp) water
- about 450 g (1 lb) sugar
- glycerin, for brushing

❖ Put the cherries, rose petals and water into a pan and bring to the boil. Cover the pan and simmer for 30 minutes, until the cherries are tender.

❖ Weigh another pan. Rub the cherry and rose-petal mixture through a sieve into this pan and note the total weight. Deduct the weight of the pan to give you the measure of the rose-scented fruit puree.

❖ Add an equivalent weight of sugar to the pan and stir over low heat until it has dissolved. Bring the preserve to the boil, then simmer it over medium heat, stirring often, for about 1 hour, or until a wooden spoon drawn through it leaves a deep channel.

❖ Brush some decorative moulds or used yoghurt pots with glycerin and spoon in the preserve. Cover with a wax disc and a jam-pot cover and leave to set. This preserve is also called 'cheese' because when it is set it has the consistency of mature cheese,

❖ Store the preserve in your equivalent to a cool Victorian larder. The preserve is best kept for at least four weeks before serving.

Makes about 550 g (1¼ lb) preserve.

ROSE-PETAL INFUSIONS

Just Desserts

From cool creamy junket sprinkled with sugar and scattered with rose petals to cherry-ring and rose-petal flan, the ways the Victorians brought the sweet fragrance of roses to the dessert table were many and varied. Rose-petal sugar, made by infusing a handful of fragrant petals in a closed jar of granulated or caster sugar, was added sparingly to give a subtle aroma to cakes and buns, creams and ice creams, sorbets and soufflés. It was a quick and easy way to add instant fragrance to a variety of dishes. Rosewater had a similar effect and was also valued by the Victorian lady as an aid to beauty.

Cherry-ring and rose-petal flan

The combination of luscious, ripe cherries and scented rose petals is delectable in any form.

> ### YOU WILL NEED
>
> ❖ 1 20-cm (8-in) flan case
> ❖ 450 g (1 lb) cherries, stoned
> ❖ 60 ml (4 tbsp) water
> ❖ 15 ml (1 tbsp) cornflour
> ❖ 30 ml (2 tbsp) redcurrant jelly
> ❖ 60 ml (4 tbsp) fragrant rose petals, torn
> ❖ velvet ribbon bow (optional)

❖ Reserve a few cherries for the decoration. Strip the remainder from the stalks and put in a pan with 45 ml (3 tbsp) of water. Bring them to the boil and simmer for 10 to 15 minutes, until they just begin to soften. Remove with a draining spoon and arrange them in the flan case.

❖ Put the remaining water in a small bowl, sprinkle on the cornflour and stir to make a smooth paste. Add this and the redcurrant jelly to the juice in the pan, and stir over medium heat until it clears and thickens. Mix in about half the rose petals.

❖ Pour the glaze over the cherries and leave until it has set. Decorate with the reserved cherries and rose petals.

Victorian junket

Junket, the ideal dairy food to serve with soft berry fruits, is made by stirring a bottled culture into warm milk and leaving it to set. The junket may then be sprinkled with sugar, cinnamon or grated nutmeg, or covered with whipped cream, and should be scattered with fragrant rose petals.

YOU WILL NEED

- 1 litre (1¾ pints) full-cream milk
- 15 ml (1 tbsp) essence of rennet
- 30 ml (2 tbsp) caster sugar, plus extra for sprinkling
- 30 ml (2 tbsp) brandy (optional)
- 150 ml (¼ pint) double cream, whipped
- powdered cinnamon or grated nutmeg (optional)
- rose petals, to decorate

❖ Heat the milk to blood heat. This is when it feels neither hot nor cold when you dip in a clean finger. On no account allow the milk to boil.

❖ Pour the warm milk into a dish and stir in the essence of rennet, the caster sugar and brandy, if you are using it. Cover the dish and set it aside for 2 hours without moving it.

❖ When the junket has set, add the topping of your choice. Arrange the rose petals in a pattern on top, and serve the dessert with, for example, strawberries sprinkled with sugar and brandy.

A bowl of ripe cherries is all the more tempting when it is decorated with a vibrant rose. Conceal a plastic water-holding phial among the fruit, to keep the flower looking fresh.

ROSEBUD POMANDER

Mingling of Aromas

ightly packed with dried rosebuds and scented with cinnamon and mace, the balls of flowers that Victorian ladies hung in their closets and above their bedheads had evolved delightfully, and through a variety of forms, from children's playthings. In ancient times young girls composed tight clusters of sturdy spring flowers such as daisies and marigolds into ball shapes to be tossed from hand to hand in springtime festivals of flora games.

Centuries later, in the Middle Ages, the 'ladies of the pot pourri', who managed the still rooms in the large houses and on the great estates, composed floral pomanders, a more decorative version of the clove oranges that were carried to scent the air and to ward off fevers.

These flower balls became popular again in the Victorian era when they had a coquettish role as well as a practical application. Ladies were wont to pick up and handle a flower pomander to release the mingled aromas, coincidentally right under the nose of a favourite beau.

Making a flower ball

In Victorian times and before, flower balls were created around a piece of wire crushed into a ball enclosing a handful of dried moss. These days, such decorations are more easily composed with the help of dry stem-holding foam (Styrofoam) balls, with the short flower stems pressed into the foam or stemless flowers attached to it edge to edge with hot glue.

YOU WILL NEED

❖ dry foam ball
❖ about 60 dried rosebuds
❖ florists' scissors
❖ 5 ml (1 tsp) dried orris-root powder
❖ 5 ml (1 tsp) ground mace
❖ 5 ml (1 tsp) ground cinnamon
❖ 5 ml (1 tsp) grated orange peel, dried
❖ medium-gauge stub wire
❖ 2.5-cm (1-in) wide ribbon

1 Cut the stems of the rosebuds to a length of about 1.5 cm (½ in). Press the rose stems into the foam so that the flowers are packed together, with no spaces in between.

2 Continue adding more dried flowers to complete the ball. Try arrangements of roses with contrasting colours to create a varied effect.

Put the orris-root powder, which fixes all the other aromas, the mace, cinnamon and orange peel into a paper bag (not a plastic one) with the rosebud ball and seal it. Toss the bag gently to cover the flowers with spices and leave it in a warm, dry place for two or three weeks, shaking it occasionally.

Remove the flower ball and shake off any spices clinging to the petals (which would give them a dusty appearance). Tie the ribbon in a bow, thread the wire through the back of the loop and press the ends into the foam.

ROSE-PETAL POT POURRI

The Aura of Victorian Times

Stir a bowl of rose-petal pot pourri with your fingers and you release not only the heady fragrance of the blend but also the aura of Victorian times. For the sweet scents of the rose garden lingered in bedrooms and drawing-rooms long after the blinds were drawn, so to speak, on the last rays of summer.

Even the names of the Bourbon and centifolia, the moss and China, Gallica and damask roses, which are still obtainable through specialist growers, evoke the romance and elegance of the age. These and many other roses provided the Victorian lady with the first essential of a summer-garden pot pourri.

Rose petals could be gathered up from beneath the scented bushes and from the brick paths that crisscrossed the rose garden. Victorian children, eager to help, might gather the petals in their pinafores or follow Mama with a shallow basket gradually filling up with pink and purple, crimson and magenta petals, some striped and others lightly flashed with a second colour.

The petals could be spread on racks covered with muslin and, on a still and sunny day, left to dry in the shade. Drying in full sun draws out the essential oils and dilutes the fragrance.

Other flowers and petals to add fragrance and colour to a pot pourri made by the dry method would be dried in a similar way or, if the weather was damp, put on shelves in the airing cupboard, to be stirred every day until they felt and sounded as dry as tissue paper.

The selection of added fragrances has always been a matter of personal preference. The only requirement is a fixative such as dried orris-root powder, to fix and hold the natural scents of the plant materials. A few drops of rose oil or another essential oil acts as an aroma reinforcement. Other additives such as ground cinnamon and allspice, nutmeg and mace are yours for the choosing.

The following recipe, typical of those favoured in Victorian times, is made by the dry pot pourri method. Another blend composed by the moist method will be found on pages 86 and 87.

1 Mix the dried plant materials together in a bowl. Add the orris-root powder, nutmeg and cinnamon, and stir the mixture thoroughly.

2 Spoon the mixture into a lidded jar and stir in the rose oil. Cover the jar and set it aside in a dry place for at least six weeks. Be sure to shake or stir the jar every day. When it is ready, use the pot pourri to fill bowls and jars, sweet bags and sachets.

YOU WILL NEED

- 1 cup dried, fragrant rose petals
- 1 cup dried lavender flowers
- 1 cup dried pansy or petunia petals
- ½ cup dried marjoram leaves
- 45 ml (3 tbsp) orris-root powder
- 2.5 ml (½ tsp) grated nutmeg
- 15 ml (1 tbsp) ground cinnamon
- 5 drops rose oil (attar of roses)

RING OF ROSES

Traditional Posy

The Victorians' love of flowers, and of roses in particular, found its prettiest and most romantic expression in the formal posy. Ring around ring of sweet-smelling flowers were composed with painstaking care to create the circular design now considered a classic of its time.

In continuation of a much earlier tradition, formal posies were carried by the bride and her attendants on her wedding day, or presented to visiting dignitaries.

Pink and red, crimson and coral were popular bridal colour themes, sometimes blended with highlights of cream or white flowers or contrasted with cool and moody blues. Such posies were destined to be practical as well as pretty, and it was the function of an outer ring of leaves or a lace or paper frill to protect the flowers.

To wire or not to wire the flowers onto false stems – that is a question that has faced floral designers from one generation to the next. There are advantages to both sides. If you do mount each flower onto a florists' stub wire and then bind it, for appearance sake, with gutta-percha (florists' tape), the flower heads can be eased and inclined this way and that. In addition, the bunch of false stems, once it is bound with satin ribbon, is likely to comprise a more slender and elegant handle.

If you retain the natural stems, you can keep the posy in water before binding the stems with ribbon.

YOU WILL NEED

❖ selection of flowers such as rosebuds,
   spray carnations, sweet peas and baby's
   breath (gypsophilia)
❖ foliage such as asparagus fern,
   maidenhair fern or variegated ivy
❖ florists' fine silver wire
❖ florists' scissors
❖ paper doily
❖ 6-mm (¼-in) wide ribbon
❖ 2.5-cm (1-in) wide ribbon

1 Separate the flowers into groups in the order in which you will use them. Hold the central flower, a rosebud, in one hand and surround it with a ring of pinks. If you wish, secure the stems at this stage by binding them with silver wire. Add short sprays of asparagus fern and baby's breath to encircle the pinks, and continue adding rings of flowers and foliage until the posy is the size you wish. Bind the stems securely with wire.

2 Cut a hole in the centre of the doily, push the stems through and bind the paper in place.

Pleat or gather it evenly around the stems, then bind them with ribbon. Tie the ribbon into a bow or a series of small bows, and leave trailing ends.

Spray the flowers with a fine mist of cool water, and place the posy in a cool, dark place. Leave it there until it is needed for that special occasion.

A SUMMER WEDDING

Here Comes The Bride

The flower compositions that greeted the Victorian bride as she progressed down the aisle on her father's arm were a study in formality and symmetry. Pedestal arrangements of peonies and roses, delphiniums and night-scented stocks would be arranged two by two on either side of a doorway, porch or arch. Windowsills would probably be adorned with a floral group at each end, in preference to a single centrally placed design, and the altar decorated with two pairs of arrangements in companion containers.

A wedding was an occasion to bring out the most formal and elegant containers the entire family could muster. Large containers such as urns and chalices in classical shapes reminiscent of the Italian Renaissance were much in favour, and they added a note of solemnity considered appropriate to the setting.

The arrangement shown here, composed in an embossed spelter urn, carries echoes of such designs. The choice of flowers, in shades ranging from deep crimson through red to pale pink and pastel mauve, is pure Victorian. The contrasting note of pale yellow, in the sprays of Peruvian lilies (alstroemeria), makes the design more in keeping with present-day preferences for lighter and brighter compositions, which can be clearly seen even in the deeper recesses of the building.

The urn is fitted with plastic-coated wire mesh netting crumpled into a ball that fits tightly into the aperture. If wire used in this way does not feel secure, and moves when it is wobbled, it should be further secured with bands of florists' adhesive tape taken over and around the wire and onto the inner rim of the container.

Composing the arrangement

YOU WILL NEED

- large urn-style container
- plastic-coated wire mesh netting
- wire cutters
- florists' adhesive tape (optional)
- selection of flowers such as carnations, lilies, pinks, orchids, roses and Peruvian lilies (alstroemeria)
- fern leaves
- florists' scissors

1 Crumble the netting into a ball to fit tightly into the top of the container. Arrange the flowers with the deepest colour, the carnations, in a wavy line from the top to the base of the design.

2 Position the large lilies to outline the top and sides of the design, then fill in the arrangement with the yellow Peruvian lilies. Arrange the roses, orchids and pinks symmetrically, and position the fern leaves to separate the groups of colour.

Spray the flowers with a fine mist of cool water. If the arrangement is to be in place for more than one day, remember to top up the container with water.

ORCHIDS AND OLD LACE

Enhancing Appearances

The mothers of the bride and bridegroom, older sisters, aunts and cousins, as well as all the principal wedding guests liked to enhance their appearance with personal flowers. A cascading spray of orchids and freesias carried by an older guest, a fulsome corsage worn on the shoulder of a beribboned gown, and a posy pinned onto or under the brim of a hat – these floral adornments were as much signs of the times as were long and elegant gloves and lace-trimmed fans.

The floral spray in the photograph, placed on a Victorian Bible, features a cascade of mauve and purple orchids, each flower cut from the main stem, mounted onto a stub wire and bound with gutta-percha (florists' tape). The orchids are arranged with wired clusters of dainty scented geranium leaves, pansies (for their romantic symbolism) and cream freesias. The natural and false stems are securely bound with fine silver wire, then tied with a strip of deep cream, mellow lace.

The corsage, which in Victorian times could have been sported by a male dandy, is composed of a deep red carnation, a cluster of pinks and sweet peas contrasted with small sprays of asparagus fern and baby's breath (gypsophilia). The natural stems are bound with fine silver wire and could be inserted in an orchid phial to give the flowers a moisture source.

A PERFECT MATCH

In the Victorian language of flowers, the pretty orchid symbolizes both a beauty or belle, and the perfect man.

The flower's exquisite scent is thought to be the 'ancestor of all fragrances'.

According to the beliefs of I Ching, the ancient Chinese fortune-telling system, if two people are of a single mind, their fused mind has the sharpness of metal and the fragrance of an orchid. Such perfect harmony, advised in the perfect marriage, is referred to as Gold Orchid.

THE BRIDE'S TABLE

A Cascade of Flowers

A cascade of flowers at the centre of the bride's table, a group of bridal-white blooms on a pedestal by the door, an elegant arrangement to create visual interest in a room corner or on a windowsill – there are many opportunities for floral compositions to adorn the setting for the wedding reception.

A wedding was one occasion when Victorian flower arrangers were likely to depart from their preference for dark toning colours and create arrangements that put the emphasis on textural rather than colour contrasts and harmonies. White and regal lilies were arranged side by side with clusters of marguerites, and full-blown cream or white roses complemented sprays of sweet-scented stephanotis.

Displayed in a two-handled metal bowl, the arrangement on these pages has echoes of those Victorian designs. White lilies arch naturally at the sides, sloping low over the handles of the container. Clusters of yellow-centred spray chrysanthemums give visual weight through the centre of the design, and carnations and roses create circles of interest on either side. Pale lemon Peruvian lilies (alstroemeria), used as filler flowers, add a warmer colour note.

Composing the arrangement

1 The polished metal bowl is fitted with plastic-coated wire mesh netting, crumpled into a ball and held in place with small strips of florists' tape. The centre of the arrangement is created with clusters of yellow-centred spray chrysanthemums. Individual flowers cut from the base of the stem are positioned around the rim of the container as an added decoration.

2 The natural curving stems of the white lilies create a downward sloping shape at the sides of the design. If some of the flowers are in bud form when you arrange them, allow space for them to open fully without crowding the other materials.

WREATHED IN ROMANCE

Clove Gillyflowers

love carnations. Gillyflowers. July-flowers. Gilloflowers. Clove gillyflowers. Call them what you will, the flowers that scented Victorian herbaceous borders and herb gardens evoke the essence of summers past, of tea on the lawn, croquet and tennis parties, and romance.

In the Victorian language of flowers, the clove gillyflower symbolized dignity, pride and unfading beauty, and the flowers were exchanged between lovers to acknowledge mutual bonds of affection. Carnations, spanning a wide colour range, had a diversity of meanings. Deep red carnations breathed the hopeless sigh that accompanied the sentiment 'Alas, for my poor heart'. Pink carnations signified a woman's love, and white ones, coyness. Yellow carnations and striped blooms were bad news, signifying, respectively, disdain and refusal. A dictionary of the time adds a note of mystery. Carnations of an unspecified colour could be preferred to symbolize fascination.

Perhaps it is helpful to turn back the pages of an earlier publication, *The Garden of Pleasant Flowers* (1629), for identification and clarification:

But what shall I say to the Queene of delight and of flowers, Carnations and Gilloflowers, whose bravery, variety and sweete smell joyned together, tyeth every one's affection . . . The names of them do differ very variably, in that names are imposed and altered as every one's fancy will have them.

Heart-shaped wreath

We have chosen to celebrate the flowers' romantic associations with a heart-shaped wreath. Suspend it on a ribbon as a wall decoration above the bed, or place it on a pile of lacy pillows. Either way, the combined scents of clove gillyflowers and rosemary (for remembrance) will create a romantic aromatherapy all their own.

YOU WILL NEED

- heart-shaped wire frame bound with ribbon
- sprays of flowering rosemary
- pinks or spray carnations
- florists' fine silver wire
- 1.5-cm (½-in) wide decorative ribbon

1 Cut short sprays of rosemary and bind them two or three at a time to the frame, so that the tips of one bunch cover the stem ends of the one before. Continue binding on stems until the shape is completely covered.

2 Make small posies of the pinks or spray carnations and bind them carefully to the rosemary wreath. Tie the ribbon into a luxurious bow, leaving trailing ends, and fix it to the base of the wreath.

SWEET AND SPICY

Gillyflower Brandy

he spicy sweetness of clove gillyflowers had been appreciated by *bon viveurs* for centuries before the Victorians discovered the experience anew. The flowers, which were also known as ratafia pinks, had been used to flavour cordials and syrups, vinegar (which was considered efficacious in the treatment of sick headaches) and wine.

An early recipe for gillyflower wine reminds us of the basic wine-making method used before chemical aids in the form of tablets and crystals were widely available. Having taken ten gallons of water and six bushels of clove gillyflowers, the amateur wine-maker was instructed to '. . . then take a crust of brown bread spread with a little ale yeast; put it in a vessel, close it until it begins to ferment, about seven days, then bottle it up with sugar and lemon peel.'

Carnations and pinks were also widely used to flavour white wine and mead, and to turn brandy and gin into aromatic digestifs to be enjoyed after a meal. The recipe that follows is adapted from one which begins, 'Take 24 pints of brandy, a pound of carnation petals and a drachm of bruised cloves.'

Crimson carnations and pinks in warm rich hues from purple to flame, these are the gillyflowers of Victorian posies and floral liqueurs.

Carnation brandy

YOU WILL NEED

❖ 1 bottle (75 cl) brandy
❖ 3 cups red or pink carnation petals,
  washed and dried if necessary
❖ 6 cloves, lightly crushed
❖ 225 g (8 oz) sugar

Pour half the brandy into another clean bottle. Pick off the white part at the base of the carnation petals and divide the petals between the two bottles. Add half the cloves and half the sugar to each bottle, put in a cork or cap and shake well.

❖ Put the bottles aside in a dry, dark place for three months, shaking them daily if possible.

❖ Strain off the liquor through a nylon sieve, pressing the petals against the sides of the sieve to extract as much flavour as possible. Pour the brandy into a clean bottle and serve as a digestif.

A HINT OF SPICE

Pot Pourri

ake one measure of nearly dried clove gillyflower petals. One measure of sweet rose petals. One half-measure of marygold petals and of the leaves of lemon verbena. Take two measures of coarse salt and make them in layers one above the other in a closed pot.'

So begins a hand-written early-Victorian recipe for moist pot pourri, the method of composing the fragrant blend of petals and leaves, spices and essential oils. The salt acts as a desiccant, drawing out the residual moisture in the plant materials, and ultimately fermenting. That is the stage at which to add the whole or powdered spices and the essential oils that evoke the very essence of a summer's garden.

You can add some ingredients purely for appearance's sake and, as the mixture matures, reinforce the colours and textures by stirring in dried peony petals or larkspur florets, coriander seeds or star anise pods.

Any recipe may serve as a general guide to proportion and fragrance strength, colour and texture rather than a hard-and-fast list of ingredients. Victorian ladies well understood how to achieve subtle or potent blends that conveyed, as sure as any bottle of perfume, their disposition and mood of the moment.

Clove gillyflower mix

YOU WILL NEED

❖ 1 cup carnation or garden pink petals
❖ 1 cup fragrant rose petals
❖ ½ cup marigold petals
❖ ½ cup verbena leaves
❖ 250 g (10 oz) coarse salt
❖ 15 ml (1 tbsp) ground allspice
❖ 30 ml (2 tbsp) orris-root powder
❖ 3 drops carnation oil
❖ 2 drops rose oil (attar of roses)
❖ 15 ml (1 tbsp) dried red peppercorns
❖ 15 ml (1 tbsp) coriander seeds
❖ 30 ml (2 tbsp) star anise pods

THE ART OF DISPLAY

Victorian ladies were divided on the most appropriate way to display pot pourri. Bearing in mind the tactile nature of the blends, and the nearly irresistible temptation to stir them with the fingers in passing, some ladies chose to scatter pot pourri in open bowls and vases, compotes and ginger jars. Fine bone china and oriental styles were much in favour, with some especially spicy mixtures displayed in wooden bowls and dishes.

Others preferred to enclose the heady charms of the mixtures in lidded jars and boxes, only occasionally lifting the lid on the fragrance, like withdrawing a veil, to provide an element of surprise.

Displaying pot pourri in open containers is considered by some to be wasteful, since in this way the fragrance is more rapidly drawn out and lost. When this eventually does happen, revive the blend by stirring in two or three drops of essential oil or a pot pourri reviver oil (from herbalists and other specialist shops).

❖ Spread the petals and leaves on wire racks covered with clean tea towels and leave them in a warm dry place such as an airing cupboard for two days, stirring them each day.
❖ Stir the plant materials together and spoon them into a wide jar or a stone crock, sprinkling salt between each layer. (Do not use a metal container of any kind.) Cover the container and set it aside for ten days, stirring the contents each day.
❖ Stir in the allspice and the fixative – the orris-root powder – and then the essential oils. Cover the container and leave it to mature for about six weeks. Stirring the jar each day during this time is aromatherapy at its most therapeutic.
❖ Stir in the spice seeds and the star anise pods and spoon the mixture into decorative containers.

THE HERB GARDEN

Scents of Occasion

Garden sage with its long spires of deep mauve flowers, and purple sage with its dark downy leaves; deep blue, straggly petalled cornflowers, brilliant blue star-shaped borage flowers and round-headed chive flowers; feathery sprays of bronze fennel and clusters of blue or purple marjoram flowers – there are so many plants and herbs of this deep dark colour range that it is tempting to bring them all together in the form of an aromatic wreath.

To make such a wreath, compose the flowers and foliage into full and compact bunches and arrange them generously, one close against the next, around a ring-form base. This makes an aromatic kitchen or wall decoration of which the Victorians would have approved. And you can leave the wreath to dry in situ.

The decoration on these pages is composed on a copper wire ring covered first with dried grasses and then bound with aubergine-coloured paper ribbon. If, as the herbs dry naturally and lose a little of their original substance, there is any show-through from the ring base, it will be sympathetic to the colour theme and seen as a continuation of the paper-ribbon bow.

Composing the herb wreath

1 Place all the flowers and foliage in a bowl of water for several hours. Cut the stems to roughly equal lengths and compose posies of mixed herbs; match, blend and contrast the colours and textures to give the decoration maximum interest and variety. Bind the posy stems with green twine and dry the stems. Bind the posies onto the paper-covered ring so that the heads of each cover the stems of the one before.

2 Unfurl a length of paper ribbon and shape it into a bow, without tying it at the centre. Cut a short length of the ribbon and, without unfurling it, wrap it around the centre of the bow. Place the bow against the ring form and twist the bow loop to attach it.

FARMER'S FRIEND

The green or bronze, feathery and misty leaves of fennel have long associations with strength. Victorious Greek warriors were decked with it, and farmers relied on its properties as an organic yield-improver. To this end, the herb was mixed with soap and salt and pressed into the hole at the head of the plough to strengthen the land and increase the volume of the crop.

FARMER'S FOE

The old country name for the cornflower was 'hurt-sicle', and derives from the time when these brilliant blue flowers were to be seen growing abundantly in the cornfields. It was said that the flowers hindered and annoyed the reapers by dulling the edges of their sickles as they worked rhythmically in line through the long fields of wheat and oats, barley and rye.

A NOSEGAY OF FLOWERS

Herb Tussie-Mussies

What romance there is in the name tussie-mussie, which describes a posy or nosegay of herbs and aromatic flowers. And yet, for all its evocation of nineteenth-century sentiments, the term has its roots far back in the Middle Ages, when judges and other dignitaries carried a herbal nosegay to sweeten the air. The herbs were selected for their perceived qualities as both disinfectant and air freshener and, with such practical necessities foremost, little thought was given to colour matching. The practice continued throughout the Victorian era (indeed it survives in some regions to this day), proving the point that carrying flowers was by no means a female prerogative.

The Victorians took this charming inheritance to their hearts and gave the tussie-mussie a style all their own. Herbal posies took their place at the dinner table, placed on a folded napkin or in a glass of water beside each place; in the kitchen, where occasionally a leaf or two might be plucked for use in cooking; and even on the fashion scene, where a tastefully chosen tussie-mussie was indistinguishable from any other posy when it was pinned to the collar of a gown or the brim of a hat.

Adapting this long-standing tradition, it is rewarding to go around the garden, or even to a well-planted windowbox, basket in hand, cutting leaves and flowers to compose these colourful and fragrant posies with the aura of ages past.

Lady's mantle (alchemilla mollis) leaves have the delightful habit of harbouring dew-drops long after other plant material has dried. In this posy, clusters of the leaves and tightly furled buds are ringed around with yellow pansies and then with fennel.

Ring the changes with variegated mint, one of the prettiest and most aromatic of herbs, surrounded by coral, pink and salmon garden pinks (gillyflowers) and an outer ring of garden mint.

Taking colour contrast to its limits, this nosegay is composed of deep blue cornflowers, chive flowers and sun-gold marigolds. It would make an especially pretty table decoration for an informal occasion.

COMPOSITION PIECE

As you compose a fragrant tussie-mussie, try taking account of the meaning ascribed to the aromatic plants in the Victorian language of flowers. You could include a sprig of marjoram to draw forth blushes, or of mint in recognition of virtue. This list will help you put your words into posies.

ANGELICA	*inspiration; magic*
BASIL, SWEET	*best wishes*
BAY	*I change but in death*
BORAGE	*bluntness*
FENNEL	*force; strength; worthy of praise*
GERANIUM, APPLE-SCENTED	*present preference*
LADY'S MANTLE	*fashion*
MARJORAM	*blushes*
MINT	*virtue*
PARSLEY	*feasting; you occupy my thoughts; festivity*
PENNYROYAL	*flee away*
PEPPERMINT	*warmth; cordiality*
ROSEMARY	*your presence revives me; remembrance*
SAGE	*esteem; domestic vitues*
SPEARMINT	*warmth of sentiment*
THYME	*activity*
WOODRUFF	*modest worth*

Just where they might grow – the tussie-mussies displayed in the herb pot include one in 'Victorian' shades of purple and pink, composed of purple sage, pink candytuft and daisy-like star of the Veldt (dimorphotheca). In another of the aromatic posies, sage leaves and chive flowers encircling a single head of deep blue bellflower (campanula) create a moody blue scheme.

A DAINTY SPREAD

Fragrant Butters

Sweet butter speckled with golden-orange marigold petals and melting into fingers of toast; rosemary-flower and clover-petal butters thinly spread in dainty heart-shaped sandwiches to pass round at a bridge tea party; slabs of butter shaped between wooden paddles and wrapped in rose petals; and parsley butter sharpened with lemon juice (known as snail butter) and drizzled over grilled meats and fish – the Victorians used a wide variety of edible flowers and aromatic herbs to enrich their golden, creamy butter.

Straight from the farm and unsalted, this rich dairy product lent itself to a wide variety of sweet and savoury embellishments. Fragrant petals or herb leaves would be finely chopped or minced and beaten into butter softened at room temperature. Larger and even more fragrant petals, especially rose and jonquil petals, were pressed into blocks of butter, wrapped in greaseproof paper and left in a cool larder for several days for their flavour to permeate. Or, like those of other edible flowers, these petals too could be chopped and mixed into the butter.

In general, butter blended with sweet-smelling flowers such as rose and violet, jonquil and carnation were served at teatime, in sandwiches or scones, on toast or toasted teacakes. Herb flowers and others with a hint of spice to them, marigold and nasturtium especially, could be used in this way or as savouries. Use nasturtium butter as a piquant condiment with grilled fish; spread clover, or melilot, butter on 'soldiers' to serve with boiled eggs.

Flower butter

This is a basic recipe for flower butter. Vary the proportions slightly according to your taste, and the strength of the aroma in the petals.

❖ Beat the lemon juice into the butter, a few drops at a time. Beat in the petals until they are evenly distributed.

❖ Shape the butter into a roll, wrap it closely in foil and store in the refrigerator for up to seven days.

❖ Allow the flavoured butter to soften at room temperature before spreading.

YOU WILL NEED

❖ 100 g (4 oz) unsalted butter, at room temperature

❖ 5 ml (1 tsp) lemon juice

❖ 60 ml (4 tbsp) edible flower petals, minced or finely chopped

Herb butter

Follow the method for making flower butter. Season the flavoured butter with salt and pepper to taste, and according to the way you intend to serve it.

❖ Shape the butter into a roll or pat it into a block and cut it in slices. To serve the butter as a garnish on meat and fish dishes, shape it into decorative pats, using small biscuit or confectionery cutters.

HERB OILS AND VINEGARS

An Array of Flavours

To the Victorian cook, the herb harvest was as important as any other harvest, a time to gather mint and tarragon, marjoram and thyme, basil, parsley, rosemary, fennel and dill to 'put down' as a flavouring for oils and vinegars. As the season progressed, the line of oil and vinegar bottles on the pantry shelves lengthened, each one containing an identifying and flavour-enhancing sprig or two of the fresh herb, and each one destined to add piquancy and interest to soups and sauces, salad dressings and gravies throughout the coming winter months .

The Victorian cook knew that if the full flavour was to be extracted from the herbs, the timing of the harvest was critical. While a sprig or so for cooking can be nipped off at any time without causing detriment to the plant, serious harvesting is quite another matter. It is best to gather the stems of the herb plants – cutting them with sharp secateurs and never pulling or breaking them off – when the flowers are in full bud, and just before they open. This is when the volatile oils, and therefore the flavour and aroma, are most concentrated.

The Victorians knew, too, that the early bird catches the plant at its most fragrant. The optimum time for harvest is early in the morning, once the dew has evaporated from the plant but before the heat of the noon-day sun draws out ever more of its volatile oils.

Herb oil

Use herb-flavoured oils in salad dressings, to add flavour when sautéing and stir-frying meat, fish and vegetables, and as the oil you pour on the turbulent water when fast-boiling rice or pasta.

YOU WILL NEED

- 1 475-ml (17-fl oz) bottle good-quality olive oil, or sunflower oil
- 6 15-cm (6-in) sprigs fresh herb, such as those mentioned above
- 2 garlic cloves, lightly crushed

❖ Pour off a little of the oil into a clean bottle and push in two of the herb sprigs and one of the garlic cloves. Top up the bottle, close it and leave it on a sunny windowsill, where it will be delightfully decorative, for two weeks. Shake the bottle once or twice a day.

❖ Remove and discard the herbs and garlic and replace them with the same quantity of fresh ones. Set aside for a further two weeks, shaking the bottle daily.

❖ Discard the herbs and garlic, pour the oil into a sterilized bottle and add the remaining sprigs of herb. Cover and store in a cool, dark place.

Herb vinegar

Make the flavoured vinegar in the way described for herb
oil and use it in salad dressings, in the court bouillon
when poaching quenelles or fish, and for pickling
vegetables. Dill vinegar, for example, is especially good
for preserving ridge cucumbers and gherkins,
traditionally known as dill pickles.

A QUIET MOMENT
Time for Tea

Camomile tea to induce peaceful sleep, lady's mantle tea to ease recurring pains, lavender tisane to ward off nervous headaches, meadowsweet tea to counter over-acidity, and clear, ruby-red hibiscus tea for the pure delight of sipping it – Victorian ladies took floral tisanes both for pleasure and for their health's sake, or at least for the perceived benefits that the infusions would bring to their well-being and state of mind. A cup of lavender tea sipped slowly in the tranquillity of her boudoir or drawing-room could do as much to relieve a lady's anxiety and calm her nerves as a sprinkling of lavender water on a lace handkerchief.

Floral and herbal tisanes are made by infusing the aerial parts of a plant, the fresh or dried flowers, petals or leaves, in boiling water just long enough to release the active constituents in the plant's volatile oils. The strained infusion may then be sweetened with honey and sipped soothingly hot or refreshingly chilled and spiked with a sliver of lime or lemon.

Victorian ladies set aside one of their prettiest teapots and their most elegant tea-strainer solely for the purpose of making these floral drinks. And, with the popular home journals of the day as a guide, they became skilled tea blenders composing, for example, an infusion of yarrow and elderflower to alleviate the after-effects of an over-indulgence in floral wines.

TISANES AND THEIR ATTRIBUTES

When a Victorian lady sipped a cup of floral tea for her health's sake, these were the benefits she hoped to reap.

Plant	Part of plant	Perceived aid for
BASIL	leaves	flatulence, nausea
CAMOMILE	flowers	insomnia
CATMINT	leaves	feverishness
CORNFLOWER	blue flowers	relief for tiredness
ELDERFLOWER	flowers	chills, fever
HYSSOP	flowers	chest complaints
LADY'S MANTLE	flowers	women's ailments
LAVENDER	flowers	nervous headaches
LEMON BALM	leaves	headaches, insomnia
LIME	flowers	headaches, indigestion
MARIGOLD	petals	indigestion
MARJORAM	flowers and leaves	asthmatic complaints
MEADOWSWEET	flowers	stomach acidity
MINT	leaves	digestive disorders
PARSLEY	leaves	indigestion
PEPPERMINT	leaves	flatulence
ROSEMARY	leaves and flowers	nervousness
SAGE	leaves	coughs and colds
THYME	leaves and flowers	colds, indigestion
YARROW	flowers	flatulence

To make floral tisanes

For each cup, measure into a warmed teapot 5 ml (1 tsp) of dried or 15 ml (1 tbsp) of fresh flowers, petals or leaves. Pour on the exact amount of boiling water required, stir, cover the pot and set it aside in a warm place to infuse for 10 minutes. Strain the tisane and enjoy it steaming hot, or allow it to cool and keep in a lidded container in the refrigerator for up to 24 hours; no more.

FLOWER CORDIALS AND SYRUPS

Fragrant Petals

Borage-flower syrup coloured the lightest shade of pale blue and swizzled with gin-based cocktails; honeysuckle syrup drizzled over dairy-rich ice cream or, flavoured with lemon juice, used as the basis for hand-churned sorbet; jasmine cordial imparting its sugary sweetness to both soft fruit salads and chilled wine cups; one could go on and on. The Victorian lady delighted in capturing the varied fragrances of her flower garden in cordials and syrups, and she knew just how to serve them, deliciously.

Recipes of the time, published in ladies' journals and in herbals and pharmacopoeias, encouraged the lady of the house to pick freely from the flower beds and herb borders, sparing little thought and, perhaps, few flowers for the morrow. Ingredient lists calling for 1.5 to 2 kg (3½ to 4 lb) of honeysuckle flowers or scarlet poppy petals were not uncommon; suggestions for scaling down the quantities were few and far between.

The flavour was extracted from the petals in two comparable and interchangeable ways. Select the one that more readily captures, for you, the flavour of the Victorian age.

Jessamine cordial

YOU WILL NEED

❖ 1 cup jasmine flowers
❖ 225 g (8 oz) caster sugar
❖ 600 ml (1 pint) boiling water

❖ Make layers of the jasmine flowers and sugar in a glass or china bowl, cover and set aside for several hours, or overnight.
❖ Pour on the boiling water, stir well, cover and leave for about 8 hours.
❖ Strain the liquid into a pan through a nylon sieve, pressing the flowers against the sides to extract as much flavour as possible.
❖ Bring the liquid to the boil and fast-boil it for 10 minutes, or until it becomes syrupy. Leave it to cool slightly, then pour into sterilized bottles, cover and label. Store in the refrigerator for up to seven days.

Honeysuckle syrup

YOU WILL NEED

❖ 1 cup honeysuckle petals
❖ 450 ml (16 fl oz) boiling water
❖ 225 g (8 oz) sugar
❖ 15 ml (1 tbsp) lemon juice

❖ Place the honeysuckle petals in a glass or china bowl and lightly bruise them to release the fragrance. Pour the boiling water onto the petals, cover the bowl and set it aside for about 4 hours.

❖ Strain the petals through a nylon sieve, pressing them against the sides to extract as much flavour as possible.

❖ Pour the flavoured liquid into a pan, add the sugar and lemon juice and stir over low heat until the sugar has dissolved. Increase the heat, bring the mixture to the boil and boil for 10 to 15 minutes, until a light syrupy consistency is reached.

❖ Cool slightly, pour into sterilized bottles, cover and label. Allow the syrup to cool, then store in a refrigerator for up to seven days.

THINKING OF THE MORROW

Drying Flowers

If you have ever wandered around a flower-filled garden and wished you could capture the form and fragrance of the blooms almost forever, then your sentiments may seem to be echoes of the past. Victorian ladies took gentle pleasure in moving from plant to plant, snipping off a handful of roses here and a few stems of many-petalled peonies there, long spires of delphinium and shorter spikes of larkspur to dry in readiness to add cheer to their homes during the dreary winter months.

Then, as now, air drying (which is described in detail on pages 130 and 131) was the most widely used method,

with desiccant drying something of a hit-and-miss affair. This more scientific method had been handed down from one generation to the next, a process that was first, it seems, discovered by accident by a housewife seeking to flavour powdered sugar with fragrant rosebuds. Successive generations adapted the method to the means available to them, using dry sand, cornmeal, borax powder and, now, lightly crushed silica gel crystals to draw out the residual moisture in the petals. Speeding up the process by heating the container of flowers and desiccant in an oven or microwave produces almost fail-proof results that would have been the envy of our Victorian ancestors.

Drying in desiccants

This method extends the range of flowers that can be successfully dried, and increases the success rate when drying, for example, fully opened roses and large peonies. Use this process for trumpet- and cup-shaped flowers, for flat, open-faced ones, and for flower sprays.

1 Spread a thin layer of crushed silica gel crystals in an ovenproof or microwave-proof container. Cut stems short and place flowers face upwards on the crystals; place sprays horizontally on the crystals.

2 Gently sprinkle on the desiccant to fill every cavity in the flower or cover every part of it, then cover it with a thin even layer of the crystals.

Place the uncovered container in an oven at the lowest temperature, or in a microwave at the lowest setting. Drying times vary according to the volume and moisture content of the plants. It is best to check their progress every minute or so, and make notes for future reference.

As a general guide, six large carnations in silica gel crystals in a cardboard shoe box may dry in a microwave in 7 minutes; a dish with a similar volume might dry in an oven with the door slightly ajar in 20 to 25 minutes.

When the flowers are dry, lift them from the desiccant, shake off any crystals clinging to the petals, and brush off any that still remain. Mount the dried flowers onto false wire stems, or use them to decorate wreaths and garlands, attaching them with hot glue or clear all-purpose glue.

FLOWERS SUITABLE FOR AIR-DRYING

Achillea	Dryandra	Peony
Astilbe	Eryngium	Rosebud
Bell heather	Feverfew	Santolina
Camomile	Golden rod	Sea lavender
Candytuft	Gypsophilia	Statice
Chive	Lady's mantle	Strawflower
Clarkia	Larkspur	Sunflower
Cornflower	Lavender	Tansy
Delphinium	Marjoram	Yarrow

LEAF CULTURE

The Height of Glory

Capturing sprays of deciduous and evergreen leaves at the height of their glory and preserving them long past their natural lifespan appealed to the Victorian lady. The simple process was a practical extension of a craft she took seriously, that of drying flowers to provide her with colourful blooms throughout the winter. Sprays of glossily preserved beech, oak and sycamore foliage complemented the usual matt texture of the flowers, making possible the textural contrasts she could achieve when arranging fresh materials.

The substance used for the preservation process was glycerin. For a decade or two an anti-freeze solution was used instead of glycerin, but it is now generally agreed that glycerin gives the most natural-looking and satisfactory results.

Harvesting

Deciduous leaves should be cut in high summer when the sap is high in the stems. This is when the solution will be most effectively carried to every part of the plant material. Evergreen leaves such as rosemary and bay can be gathered throughout the year, except in early spring when tender, young green shoots are appearing. Bracts such as bells of Ireland should be cut before they start to dry on the plant (when their colour fades). Sprays bearing hips and berries, such as glossy red rosehips and juicy blackberries, should be cut when the fruit is fully ripe. It will lose only a little of its tempting appearance in the preservation process.

Preparation

Pick over your selected material and discard any damaged leaves or bracts, and pick off any broken stems. Scrape off the bark from the ends of woody stems such as rose and lime to a depth of about 5 cm (2 in), and split or lightly crush the stem ends. This will enable them to take up the solution more easily into the foliage.

The preserving process

Make up a solution of one part glycerin, which you can buy from chemists, and two parts very hot water. Mix thoroughly, and pour to a depth of about 5 cm (2 in) in a heatproof container. Stand the stems in the solution, making sure the ends are submerged, and leave them for up to three weeks in a light, dry room. The material is preserved when beads of the solution appear on the surface of large leaves, or when the material is supple and shows no sign of brittleness.

Storing

When the leaves have been preserved, wipe them and the stems with a damp cloth to remove any stickiness. Store them, loosely arranged, in a dry container or between sheets of kitchen paper in a box in a cool, dry place.

Strain the left-over solution to remove any particles of bark, then store it in a covered jar. The solution can be used again if reheated.

Sprays of beech and copper beech, hawthorn and sycamore, rose and hellebore leaves, the latter complete with undeveloped seedpods, will provide glowing contrast to dried flowers in arrangements throughout the winter.

PART THREE

As Summer Ends

As shadows lengthen and the fragrant summer flowers fade, there comes a time to harvest and conserve the mellow fruits of the new season, to turn holiday mementoes into lasting keepsakes and make preparations for the approaching festivals. From gentle aids to beauty to sparkling celebration drinks, glowing store-cupboard preserves to stylish designs for the home, these are the ways the Victorian lady put flowers to practical and decorative use.

TRAVEL NOTEBOOK

A Journey through Europe

When one Victorian lady, Ada Mary Ann Brown, set out from home on her first voyage to Europe in 1871, she took with her all she needed to make her own special travel journal in pressed flower cameos – a small pair of scissors, a pair of wooden tweezers, a camel-hair paintbrush and a thick, leather-bound album.

Wherever the train set her down for an overnight stay, or she rested by a river or in the gardens of a villa, she captured the colours and the scents around her by picking a few leaves and wild flowers and composing them on the page into simple groupings, to be stuck in place with a light animal-based glue on her return, once they were thoroughly dry. As the mood took her, or the plant materials inspired her, she arranged them into geo-metrical shapes, one-dimensional posies and bouquets, colour co-ordinated floral patchworks and collages, and sometimes even shaped tiny petals or leaflets into words that made an identifying caption unnecessary. Tiny maidenhair fern leaflets, for example, were painstakingly arranged to spell out Tivoli, and forget-me-not flowers to form the name of the medieval Italian town Gubbio.

With sheets of flimsy paper interleaved throughout the book, and with the weight of her luggage pressing heavily down on the album throughout the journey, Ada Mary Ann's pressed flower notebook became a lasting memento of an adventurous Victorian lady's solitary travels among the flowers and foliage of Europe.

1 *On leaving home.* Mallow, *mildness. And little*
calendula, *sun bright.*

2 *St Malo, early morning, from the balcony.* Wine-red
fuschia, *taste, and* London pride, *for frivolity.*

3 *Flanders, beyond the fields of flax.* Gillyflowers, *dignity.*
Bell flowers, *constancy, and purple dried* hydrangea.

4 *Coblenz, for a day's Rhine roaming.* Fritillaries. Lilies.
Adonis amurensis *(pretty name) and* African daisy.

5 *Lake Lucerne, from the walls of a villa. Ivy and* peony leaves. *Pansies. And pearly white* everlasting flowers. *Constancy and simplicity.*

6 *Villa d'Este, Como. A surprise. Physalis, sun-orange globes. And* wild daisies. *To fill a book with them!*

7 *Florence, my face sprayed with the scent of flowers. Pulsatillas in every colour. They mean 'without pretension.'*

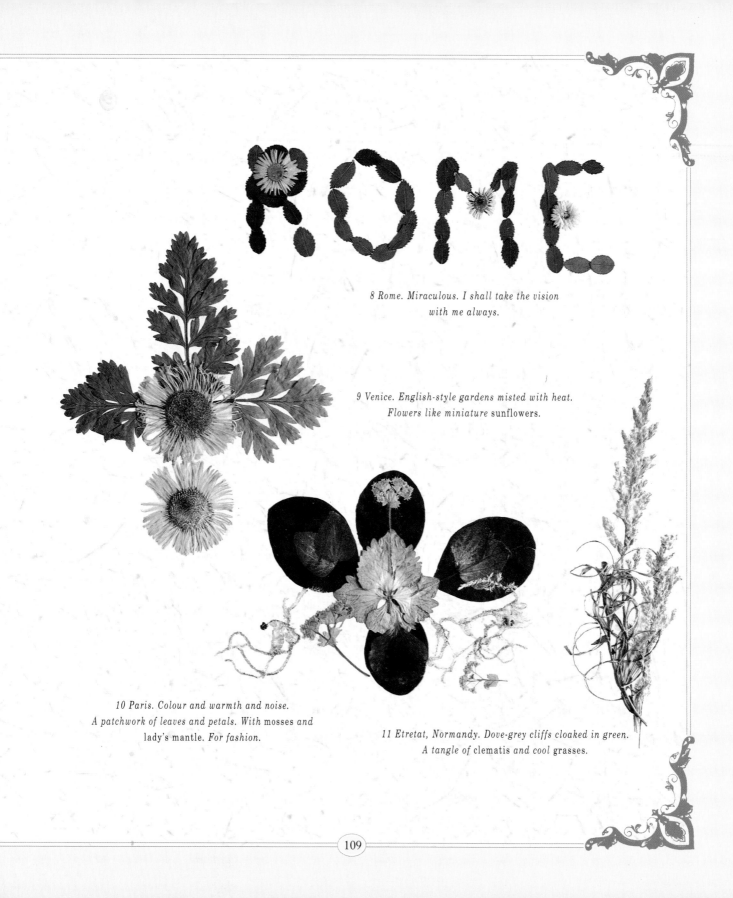

ROME

8 Rome. Miraculous. I shall take the vision
with me always.

9 Venice. English-style gardens misted with heat.
Flowers like miniature sunflowers.

10 Paris. Colour and warmth and noise.
A patchwork of leaves and petals. With mosses and
lady's mantle. For fashion.

11 Etretat, Normandy. Dove-grey cliffs cloaked in green.
A tangle of clematis and cool grasses.

MY LADY'S BOUDOIR

Floral Waters

The Victorian lady's flower garden provided her with a rich harvest of fragrant materials from which she could compose floral waters and splashes, cosmetic creams and soaps, hair preparations and other blends to enhance her bath-time experience. Lavender and marigolds, camomile and roses, lady's mantle and thyme – these and other flowers and leaves played a gentle part in filling the silver-topped bottles and lace-edged shelves in my lady's boudoir.

Lavender and rosemary skin freshener

Lavender and rosemary have a cleansing, stimulating and toning effect on the skin.
Splash this lotion on the face after cleansing and before applying a moisturizer.

YOU WILL NEED

❖ 60 ml (4 tbsp) lavender flowers
❖ 60 ml (4 tbsp) rosemary flowers, or crumbled rosemary leaves
❖ 300 ml (½ pint) distilled water

❖ Put all the ingredients in a small enamel or heatproof glass pan, cover and bring slowly to the boil. Remove from the heat and leave the infusion for 1 hour. Strain off the flowers and leaves, pressing them against the sieve. Pour into a bottle, label it and close it with a stopper.

Marigold lotion

Astringent, cleansing, toning and healing, marigold lotion helps give the skin the delicate look that was the Victorian lady's ideal.

YOU WILL NEED

❖ 2 cups marigold petals
❖ strip of thinly pared orange rind
❖ 300 ml (½ pint) distilled water

❖ Put all the ingredients into a small enamel or heatproof glass pan, cover and bring slowly to the boil. Simmer gently for 10 minutes, remove from the heat and set aside to infuse for about 1½ hours.
❖ Strain off the petals and orange rind, pressing them against the sieve to extract as much fragrant oil as possible. Pour into a bottle, label it and close it with a stopper.

Floral splash

Combine the myriad scents of a selection of country-garden flowers in this soothing and cooling splash.

YOU WILL NEED

* 4 cups fragrant flowers or petals such as camomile, lady's mantle, lavender, marigold, rose and violet
* 600 ml (1 pint) distilled water
* 45 ml (3 tbsp) vodka

❖ Place all the ingredients in a heatproof glass jar or other container with a close-fitting lid. Stand the container on a pad of newspaper or cloth in a deep pan and pour on water to come almost to the top of the jar. Bring to the boil and keep at a steady, rolling boil for 30 minutes. Remove the container from the pan and set aside in a warm, sunny place for three weeks, shaking it once or twice a day.

❖ Strain off the flowers, pressing them against the sieve. Pour the fragrant liquid into a bottle, label and close it with a stopper. Store in a cool place, away from strong light.

Rosewater

True rosewater is the gently fragrant by-product of the distillation process by which the essential oil is extracted from the petals. It may be added to bathwater or to rinsing water for the hair.

YOU WILL NEED

* 5 cups fragrant rose petals
* 300 ml (½ pint) distilled water
* 2.5 ml (½ tsp) liquid storax
* 2.5 ml (½ tsp) tincture of benzoin

❖ Put all the ingredients into a small enamel or heatproof glass pan, cover tightly with foil and then with the lid. Bring slowly to the boil, lower the heat and simmer very gently over a heat diffuser for 1½ hours. Remove the pan from the heat and leave it to infuse for 48 hours.

❖ Return the pan to the lowest possible heat, bring to the boil and simmer for a further hour. Remove from the heat and set aside to cool.

❖ Strain off the petals, pressing them against the sieve to extract the last drop of moisture. Pour into a bottle, label it and close it with a stopper.

SCENTED SOAP

Victorian Aromatherapy

atmeal and rosemary-flower honey soap, marigold-petal washballs and lavender flower soap – these and other fragrant soaps made their contribution to Victorian aromatherapy in the boudoir or the bathroom even before they played their part in keeping m'lady's skin smooth and soft.

To make scented soap, the Victorians neutralized caustic soda with a variety of vegetable and nut oils, coconut oil especially. It is a process now recognized as being messy and fraught with difficulties, so a safer, gentler method is recommended: these recipes both for soap balls and liquid soap are made with grated pure Castile soap, scented with crushed flowers and essential oils.

Lavender-flower soap

YOU WILL NEED

❖ 150 ml (10 tbsp) grated pure Castile soap
❖ 15 ml (1 tbsp) lavender honey (see page 166)
❖ 15 ml (1 tbsp) lavender-flower water (see pages 110 and 111)
❖ 30 ml (2 tbsp) dried lavender flowers, pounded

❖ Melt the soap and honey in the lavender water in a container over a pan of simmering water. Remove from the heat, add crushed lavender flowers and form the soapballs. Place them on greaseproof paper and leave in a warm, dry place for two weeks.

Marigold-petal washballs

YOU WILL NEED

❖ 150 ml (10 tbsp) grated pure Castile soap
❖ 10 ml (2 tsp) honey
❖ 30 ml (2 tbsp) marigold lotion (see pages 110 and 111)
❖ 30 ml (2 tbsp) dried marigold petals, pounded

❖ Melt the soap and honey in the marigold lotion in a container over a pan of simmering water. Remove the container from the heat, stir in the crushed marigold petals and form the soap into balls. Place the soapballs on greaseproof paper, and leave to harden in a warm, dry place for two weeks.

Rose-petal pouring soap

YOU WILL NEED

- 150 ml (10 tbsp) grated pure Castile soap
- 100 ml (4 fl oz) rosewater (see pages 110 and 111)
- 2.5 ml (½ tsp) olive oil
- 30 ml (2 tbsp) pounded dried rose petals
- 4 drops rose oil

❖ Melt the soap in the rosewater in a heatproof container over simmering water. Remove from the heat and stir in the olive oil one or two drops at a time. Stir in the pounded rose petals and the rose oil and mix well.

❖ Pour the liquid soap into a bottle, label, and close it with a stopper.

Oatmeal and honey soap

YOU WILL NEED

- 150 ml (10 tbsp) grated Castile soap
- 30 ml (2 tbsp) water
- 2.5 ml (½ tsp) walnut oil
- 15 ml (1 tbsp) rosemary-flower honey or other flower-scented honey (see pages 166 and 167)
- 30 ml (2 tbsp) medium oatmeal, soaked in water and squeezed dry

❖ Melt the grated soap in the water in a heatproof bowl over a pan of simmering water, or in a microwave-proof container in a microwave at the lowest setting. Stir in the walnut oil, one or two drops at a time, then stir in the honey and, when it has been absorbed, the oatmeal. Stir well and set aside to cool.

❖ Shape the soap into balls between the palms of your hands and place them on a baking sheet lined with greaseproof paper. Leave in a warm, dry place until the soap has set hard; this may take up to two weeks. When the soap has set, polish it with a clean, soft cloth and carefully smooth any rough edges.

A SECRET DEBT

Floral Shampoos and Rinses

hether a Victorian lady's hair was twisted into a knot, tucked under a lace-edged cap or, on more intimate occasions, allowed to fall around her shoulders, the condition of her long tresses usually owed a secret debt to flowers and herbs from her garden. Making hair-care preparations was a craft that mothers taught their daughters, ensuring that the secret of having beautiful hair was passed from one generation to the next.

The golden tints of a camomile infusion brought out the natural highlights in fair hair; whereas the copper-bronze colouring of marigold-petal infusion emphasized the glory of auburn locks. A herbal rinse made with comfrey, rosemary, sage or thyme leaves was relied upon to strengthen the colour of dark hair; and an infusion of comfrey or marshmallow was used to bring back a healthy glow to dry hair. Conversely, lavender flowers were infused as a revitalizing rinse for greasy hair.

Lavender shampoo

This soapless shampoo utilizes the protein in the egg yolks to enrich dry hair.

You Will Need

❖ 60 ml (4 tbsp) lavender water (see pages 110 and 111)
❖ juice of 2 lemons
❖ 3 eggs

❖ Whisk all the ingredients together and, if you make up the shampoo in advance, store it in the refrigerator.
❖ Massage the shampoo well into the hair, rinse, and apply the shampoo again. Rinse thoroughly.

Camomile shampoo

This creamy liquid shampoo is recommended for fair hair, and for any dry condition.

You Will Need

❖ 45 ml (3 tbsp) dried camomile flowers
❖ 1 litre (1¾ pints) boiling water
❖ 60 ml (4 tbsp) grated pure Castile soap
❖ juice of ½ lemon

❖ Put the flowers and water into a bowl, stir and cover. After 2 hours, strain into a heatproof bowl over a pan of simmering water. Add the soap and lemon juice, stir until the soap has melted. Whisk the shampoo and bottle it.

Marigold and yarrow rinse

Used after shampooing, this hair rinse had a dual purpose, to combat greasiness and control dandruff.

YOU WILL NEED

- ❖ 1 cup marigold flowers
- ❖ 1 cup yarrow flowers
- ❖ 1 litre (1¾ pints) white vinegar or cider vinegar

❖ Put the flowers into a large lidded jar, pour on the vinegar and close the jar. Leave it in a warm place – a sunny windowsill is ideal – and shake it every day for a week. Strain off the flowers, pour the rinse into bottles, label them and cover them with stoppers.

❖ Add about 150 ml (5 fl oz) of the floral rinse to the water for the final rinse after washing your hair.

MY LADY'S BATHROOM

Fragrant Infusions

he Victorian lady drew few distinctions between the floral and herbal infusions in her larder and those in her bathroom. Indeed, many bottles of aromatic oils and vinegars were duplicated in both quarters. Pot pourri led a double life, too. Mixtures made up for display in the drawing-room were equally appropriate for use as strewing herbs, or for putting up in 'sweet bags' to be swished and swirled about in the bathwater.

Simple flower and water infusions also played a dual role. They were both sipped slowly and leisurely as soothing tisanes and poured into the bath to make that, too, a haven of relaxation. A list of the supposed benefits of these bath-time infusions is given below.

Floral and herbal vinegars were added to the water in the bath so that the acidity could counteract dryness in the skin, and aromatic oils were added in small quantities, of about 15 ml (1 tbsp) to soothe and stimulate the skin.

The concept of scattering rose petals, or jasmine flowers, or marigold petals on the surface of the water may be a romantic one. But the dénouement is less so, when one emerges from the bath with damp, confetti-like particles clinging to the skin. A practical alternative is to hang a Victorian-style posy of herbs and scented flowers beneath the hot tap, and then to regulate the water to a gentle flow.

Another way is to compose a fragrant and cleansing sweet mixture, a close relative of rose-petal pot pourri, and tie it into squares of muslin or, more romantically, into lace-edged doilies. These can be used over and over again with fresh variations of the mixture, each one evoking the pampered tranquillity of the Victorian bathroom.

Bath infusions

Make these infusions by steeping a cup of flowers, petals or leaves in 1½ litres (2½ pints) of boiling water for one hour, stirring occasionally. Strain and bottle the infusion and add about 300 ml (½ pint) to the bathwater.

Plant	Perceived effect
CAMOMILE FLOWERS	*relaxing, cleansing*
ELDER FLOWERS	*refreshing, cleansing*
HYSSOP FLOWERS	*relaxing*
LAVENDER FLOWERS	*relaxing, cleansing*
LEMON VERBENA LEAVES	*skin tonic*
ROSEMARY LEAVES AND FLOWERS	*stimulating*
SWEET BASIL LEAVES	*skin tonic*
VALERIAN FLOWERS	*relaxing, soothing*
YARROW FLOWERS	*skin tonic*

Sweet-bag bath mixture

The addition of oatmeal to this pot-pourri-like mixture gives it an extra cleansing property. You may if you wish rub one of the bags onto your damp skin, using a gentle, circular motion.

❖ Mix together the rose petals, lavender flowers and oatmeal and stir in the rose oil one drop at a time. Spoon the mixture into a lidded jar, close the lid and set it aside for at least a week, for the aroma to mature. Shake the jar every day.

❖ Spoon the mixture into sweet bags and tie them with ribbons or lace.

YOU WILL NEED

❖ 1 cup dried fragrant rose petals, torn
❖ ½ cup dried lavender flowers, crushed
❖ 1 cup medium oatmeal
❖ 2 drops rose oil

SEASIDE MEMENTOES

Ring-A-Ring of Seashells

Colourful seaside buckets piled to overflowing with a motley collection of sand-covered seashells and shiny pebbles; baskets filling up with windswept seashore flowers and sun-dried clumps of knobbly seaweed; pieces of exotic-looking coral tantalizingly on sale in specialist shops – these are the kinds of thing that Victorian seaside holiday memories were made of.

This was the age when parents and children took the fun of beachcombing seriously, when holiday mementoes and treasure trove were as important a part of the enjoyment of the holiday as the family photograph album. Washed, scrubbed and dried, the shells were mounted on boards or framed in cases in the manner of needlework samplers. Or they might have been arranged in glass jars, with layers of tritons and chitons, cowries and conches, whelks and wentletraps forming a fascinating kaleidoscope of marine life. Shell collages were popular too; patchworks of contrasting colours and shapes glued onto plates and dishes or around old picture and mirror frames gave them a new lease of decorative life.

The memento wreath

꧁ ✳ ꧂

The memento wreath in the photograph captures the spirit of Victorian shellcraft of this kind, bringing together the collected elements of seashore and sand dune. The wreath form is one of twisted twigs, readily available now in florists' shops and department stores. Short-stemmed bunches of sea lavender are bound with fine silver wire and attached to the ring, facing this way and that, with bent stub wires. Short, straggly pieces of sea coral are attached to the base in a similar way, their natural curves following the outline of the ring. A dried globe artichoke head is wired to the base as a central feature, its spiky form echoed in two golden yellow thistles.

Clusters of shells attached with glue complete the design, creating a build-up of bivalves and gastropods that might have been washed up on the beach at low tide.

SHADES OF ELEGANCE

Parasols and Straw Hats

Along with the parasol and picnic basket, the wind-break and the beach towels, Victorian ladies heading for the beach would not set out without the added protection of a wide-brimmed hat. Both fashion and propriety decreed that a fair, unblemished skin was the ultimate goal; palest porcelain 'the look'.

It was generally accepted that the seaside holiday was part of 'the season' and that the rows of beach huts and deck-chairs were part of the fashion scene. In this setting, hats were pretty as well as practical; their trailing ribbons and posies of dried and artificial flowers were as much in evidence on the promenades as they were on country-house lawns.

Seashore hat

Our interpretation of this topical elegance is a full-brimmed straw hat trimmed with a wide, shimmering ribbon band and a decoration of exotic seedheads and craggy seashells. The overall colour scheme is restrained, in contrast to the exuberance of the design and the slight eccentricity of the concept.

Both a hot glue gun and clear all-purpose adhesive make light work of a decoration of this kind. Uneven strands of dusky-pink coral are pulled from the stem, bound into clusters with fine silver wire and glued into place, one facing in each direction. Shells chosen within the browny-pink colour range are glued seemingly at random around the coral, leaving ample space for the flower trim.

Each seedhead, like a two-toned, trumpet-shaped flower, is embellished with a pale pink, daisy-like strawflower glued deep inside the cavity. The seedheads (imported from South America and available from some florists) are glued in place to complete the unusual posy-like decoration. And to turn the heads of bathing and beachcombing beaux.

HOW DOES YOUR GARDEN GROW?

With Cockle Shells

Victorians who, as children, grew up chanting the evocative nursery rhyme about 'silver bells and cockle shells' were apt in later life to put the romantic concept into practice. The textural contrast between ridged and craggy, polished and patterned shells and delicate flowers, referred to in the rhyme as 'pretty maids all in a row' touched a romantic chord for the Victorian lady who liked to plant an indoor garden for display in her breakfast-room or morning-room. The idea appealed to generations of children, too, who loved to plant their own memento gardens with a handful of shells collected on a seaside outing.

Shells could enhance an indoor garden in two ways. Those of architectural proportions, such as tritons, large turrids and conch shells, could be used as marine statuary – stately figures positioned at focal points among low-growing plants. Other, flatter shells, such as cockles, clams and limpets, could be laid one over the other as a seashore collage, providing effective ground cover and an attractive visual contrast to trails of foliage.

Perhaps the prettiest shell-garden planters, and those most favoured by the Victorians, were more of the same – large deep shells with apertures wide enough to contain a group of compact and low-growing plants. These could be alpines, perennial herbs or compact indoor flowering plants such as kalanchoe, which is a colourful succulent that has yellow, pink or crimson flowers all year round.

The large, fan-shaped shell was planted with a golden thyme, trails of ground ivy, and calluna vulgaris 'Spring Cream', a type of heather that has light cream tips.

Planting a shell garden

Whether you choose a large shell or ornamental bowl as a planter, put in a handful of gravel or small stones to provide a drainage facility, and then a thin layer of crushed charcoal, which will help to keep the growing medium 'sweet'. Any general-purpose potting compost is suitable, but never use soil dug up from the garden. Choose between a peat-based or a loam-based potting compost.

Arrange the plants temporarily on the surface of the container and check that the grouping is attractive from all viewing angles. Release each plant from its original

The deep green pottery bowl is planted with a red-flowering succulent, kalanchoe, two ballota plants with contrasting golden and silver-grey foliage, ground ivy and Calluna vulgaris 'Tricolorfolia', which has pale lavender flowers in late summer.

pot, trying to keep a ball of compost intact around the roots. Firm the compost around each plant as you insert it, and lightly water the surface with a fine spray.

Now for the 'cockle shells' element of the rhyme. Position any feature shells, or a patchwork of ground-cover ones, and brush off any soil particles that cling to them.

MELLOW FRUITFULNESS

Pure Temptation

hallow, paper-padded baskets laden with thick bunches of luscious black and white grapes that have been cut, still sun-warmed, from the glasshouse. Pedestal dishes arranged with late-summer flowers and an opulence of grapes, the clusters spilling over the rims as a symbol of irresistible temptation. A ring of grapes and full-petalled roses composed as a wall or table decoration, a sign of friendship and welcome, richness and plenty, and the luxury of a bountiful harvest. The Victorians well understood the voluptuous appeal of heavy clusters of grapes and exploited it, visually, to the full.

A wreath heavy with grapes and flowers is perhaps one of the most evocative and decorative ways to recapture that concept. You could place it centre-table at a harvest supper or a wine reception; hang one above a buffet table as a sure sign of plenty or, more romantically, above a bedhead.

A small pair of Victorian silver grape scissors placed close to the decoration would provide the wherewithal for midnight feasting, which would in time reveal more of the structure of the wreath. But that would be no bad thing, because the wreath form is entirely appropriate, composed of intertwined vine twigs bound with more of their kind.

A wreath heavy with grapes

The grapes are held securely in place with heavy-gauge stub wires, taken several times around the stem of each bunch and through the wreath form, to be twisted and bent back on the reverse.

The roses are chosen to form a perfect partnership with the grapes, both visually and with a practical connotation. Generations of vintners have planted rose bushes at each end of their rows of vines, as a warning against an invasion of rust or pest (on the assumption that the rose bushes would be attacked first). Both roses and the rust-coloured blackberry leaves are attached to the ring asymmetrically, and with lighter wires.

SWEET MARY-GOLDES

Capturing the Imagination

The bright sunshine-gold marigold flowers have captured the imagination of writers and cooks through the ages. The habit of the flowers to open and close their eyes with the coming up and the going down of the sun prompted Shakespeare's lines in *Cymbeline*:

> *Hark! Hark! the lark at heaven's gate sings*
> *And Phoebus 'gins arise . . .*
> *And winking Mary-buds begin*
> *To ope their golden eyes . . .*

John Gerard (1545-1612), in his book *Herball*, noted the country name for the flower, 'Jackanapes-on-horse-backe', which so delighted Victorian children, and set out medicinal and culinary uses for the plant that inspired future generations.

By Victorian times, it would have been possible to enjoy dishes from early morning to night that were enlivened with the spicy flavour and the brilliant colour of the flowers. Scrambled eggs seasoned with nutmeg and marigold petals for breakfast; clear chicken broth scattered with the petals to precede a mixed meat salamagundy salad decorated with the flowers for luncheon; marigold buns and the flower jelly drizzled on toast at teatime; and beef and marigold stew and marigold rice pudding for supper. For the drinks trolly, there could be a selection of marigold wine, cordial or liqueur, and for sweetmeat, fondants tastefully decorated with candied petals.

Our recipe is for marigold pudding, a hearty dessert in the Victorian fashion, which is speckled with petals stirred into the mixture and decorated with whole flowers. You could serve it with custard sauce.

Coral-coloured roses and bright orange marigolds
make an enchanting country-style posy.

Marigold pudding

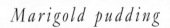

SERVES 6

❖ Sift the flour into a bowl, beat in the margarine and sugar, the eggs and the orange rind and juice. Stir in the marigold petals.

❖ Grease a 900 ml (1¾ pint) heatproof bowl and spoon in the mixture. Level the top, cover it with filmwrap and cook in a microwave on high power for 6 to 7 minutes.

❖ Alternatively, cover the bowl with greased greaseproof paper and a cloth and steam it for 1½ hours.

❖ Turn the pudding out onto a serving plate, decorate it with flowers and serve hot.

YOU WILL NEED

❖ 150 g (6 oz) self-raising flour
❖ 100 g (4 oz) soft margarine, plus extra for greasing
❖ 100 g (4 oz) caster sugar
❖ 2 eggs, beaten
❖ grated rind and juice of 2 small oranges
❖ 60 ml (4 tbsp) marigold petals, washed and dried if necessary
❖ marigold flowers, to decorate

A BOUNTIFUL HARVEST

Flower and Herb Jellies

As willow baskets filled with prolific varieties of cooking apples were brought into the Victorian kitchen, family recipe books were consulted to turn a bountiful harvest into a selection of preserves that would enliven winter menus – lavender jelly to spread meltingly onto toasted teacakes and muffins; marigold jelly to serve with scones or on cinnamon toast; rose-petal jelly to use as a filling for sponge sandwich cakes; and hibiscus jelly to spread sparingly on thin slices of brown bread and butter. Herb jellies – parsley, scented geranium, coriander, mint, sage and others – add fragrance and flavour to a basic recipe for apple jelly and are delectable when served with meats or fish.

As a general rule, flower-scented jelly preserves are made by infusing fresh or dried flowers or petals with the fruit as it is cooked, and then for further colour and flavour, adding flower petals tied in a piece of muslin as the preserve is boiled to setting point. A few extra petals may be stirred into the jelly, before it is potted.

Herb jellies are usually infused with the fragrant leaves at both stages, and chopped fresh leaves stirred in just before the preserve is poured into warmed jars.

Testing time

To test when the jelly preserve has reached setting point, remove the pan from the heat and spoon a little of the syrupy liquid onto a cold saucer. Leave it to cool, then push a finger across the surface. If the jelly wrinkles, it is ready to pour into jars. If it does not, bring the preserve back to the boil and test again after 3 or 4 minutes.

Apple and herb jellies

Make the herb-flavoured jellies in the manner described for flower preserves. Infuse 4 or 5 large sprays of the herb at each stage of the cooking and, if you wish, stir in about 60 ml (4 tbsp) chopped herbs.

VICTORIAN VARIETY

The Victorian cook was spoilt for choice in the range of apples available to her. These are a few of the evocative names from a grower's handbook at the time. *Blenheim Orange, Gloria Mundi, Golden Noble, Lane's Prince Albert, Queen, Reinette du Canada, Tower of Glamis, Transparent de Croncels, Venus Pippin, Victory.*

Apple and flower jellies

Flavour this basic jelly preserve recipe with any edible and fragrant flowers you please (see list on pages 26 and 27) to turn it into a Victorian delicacy.

YOU WILL NEED

❖ 1 kg (2¼ lb) cooking apples
❖ juice of 2 lemons
❖ 1 litre (1¾ pints) water
❖ 60 ml (4 tbsp) dried edible flowers or petals,
   or 120 ml (8 tbsp) fresh flowers or petals
❖ about 750 g (1½ lb) sugar

❖ Put the apples into a large pan with the lemon juice and water. Add half the flowers or petals and bring slowly to the boil.

❖ Boil gently for 20 to 30 minutes, until the apples have collapsed.

❖ Wring out a cotton, muslin or traditional flannel jelly bag in hot water and suspend it over a large bowl. Spoon in the fruit and liquid and leave to drain, undisturbed, for several hours. Do not squeeze the bag, as this will make the jelly cloudy.

❖ Measure the strained fruit juice and return it to the pan. Add 450 g (1 lb) sugar to each 600 ml (1 pint) of juice. Add the remaining flowers or petals, tied in a piece of muslin. Stir over low heat until the sugar dissolves, then increase the heat and boil rapidly for 10 minutes, or until setting point is reached (see p. 128).

❖ Remove the muslin bag, pour the preserve into clean, warm jars, cover and label. Store in a cool, dark place.

A SECOND FLOWERING

Harvesting Seedheads

ictorian ladies appreciated the decorative value of poppy heads and love-in-a-mist, Chinese lanterns and teasels too much to allow the gardener to whisk the seedheads off in their prime, only to moulder on the compost heap. In Victorian times, effective and efficient desiccants were unknown and flower-drying techniques were therefore far from reliable, so keen flower arrangers garnered and dried a variety of seedheads to give substance and form to their over-wintering decorations.

Seedheads could be left to begin the natural drying process on the plants, at least in a fine spell of weather, and brought indoors to continue it in the warm, dry atmosphere of a boiler-room or heated greenhouse.

What seedheads – with the exception of Chinese lanterns – lack in terms of strong colour, they compensate for in their variety of shapes and textures. There are the green-going-on-purple classical urn shapes of poppy heads; the creamy green and ridged near-spherical carriers of love-in-a-mist seeds, each one encased in a crisscrossing mesh of bright green fibres; the spiky, architectural ovals of teasel that, once the tiny mauve flowers have scattered on the wind, are deep, rich beige; and the pairs of grey velvety seedpods that span a lupin stem. Seedheads such as these can be arranged, as they

were in Victorian times, to jostle animatedly together to compose a long-lasting group that the changing light throws into fascinating relief.

The Victorians loved to use ornamental and common grasses in their arrangements; indeed, it seems almost as if they discovered their decorative use. And so their winter compositions, as lovely as they were long-lasting, shimmered with the movement of quaking grass and wallowed in the furry depth of hare's-tail grass. Grasses and dried cereals, when closely packed together with other seed carriers, added a further dimension in groupings that were so dense and deep as to be irresistibly tactile.

Harvesting and drying seedheads

Leave the seedheads on the plants until they have begun to dry and, if possible, have shed their seeds to ensure the following year's harvest. Cut the stems on a dry day and when any dew has dried out.

Tie them into bunches, a few in each, with the seedheads ranged at varying heights, and hang them in a warm, dry room where they will have free circulation of air. If it is more convenient, you can arrange the stems in dry, wide-necked containers so that the heads splay outwards and air can readily circulate around them.

The brilliance of the orange Chinese lantern seedheads contrasts dramatically with the soft creamy-brown and beige of the ornamental grasses and other seed carriers.

Seedheads to dry

Emulate our Victorian ancestors and build up a varied collection of dried seedheads. These are a few examples to dry.

Plant material	Characteristics
ERYNGIUM	Clusters of oval, thistle-like shapes irregularly borne on branching stems
GLOBE THISTLE	Almost spherical heads with a blue-purple tinge
HONESTY	When the seedheads are dry, rub off the two outer membranes to reveal the translucent silvery interior discs
JERUSALEM SAGE	Composite flower-like shapes, creamy beige on long erect stems
MALLOW	The seedheads, like silvery stars, are borne at close intervals on the long, rigid stems
MILLET	Long stems of minute reddish-brown seedheads in a brush-like formation
ORNAMENTAL ONION	Creamy-brown stemlets form a fan shape, each one topped with a small brown star
RUE	The clusters of chestnut-brown seed-pods are exquisite, like miniature wood carvings

EMMA'S CHRISTENING
Gift Basket

he announcement has been published in the newspapers, proclaiming the birth of Emma Jane Elizabeth, a sister for William Joseph. The second tier of the proud parents' wedding cake has been checked over, and a sugar-paste cradle filled with pink roses arranged in the centre, in celebration of the new baby's baptism. Uncles and other members of Emma's extended family have taken stock of their wine cellars and brought out a bottle or two considered appropriate to the occasion, and aunts and female cousins have taken up their needlework, knitting and crochet with new purpose.

One of them, renowned for her beautiful garden and her love of flowers, started cutting some of her finest blooms as soon as word reached her of Emma's birth. Her memento of the baby's baptism day, a gift that will give pleasure to the child's mother for many months to come, is a deep painted basket filled with a profusion of dried flowers in a colour range from softest baby pink to nearly purple.

Most of the flowers – the pink and blue larkspur, blue and purple hydrangea, fragrant lavender, strawflowers, carthamus and tightly furled rosebuds – have been air-dried by hanging in bunches in a warm, dry room. Others – large, showy heads of peony and pink, crimson and magenta zinnias – have had the moisture gradually drawn from their petals by a desiccant. Then, when completely dry, each of these flowers has been taped onto a length of split cane, a false stem that is easily concealed among the mass of natural stems and flowers.

The willow basket was painted a deep, old-rose pink and would in Emma's day have been filled with dry moss to keep the flower stems in directional order.

1 The most eye-catching flowers in the arrangement, the peonies, are arranged first, the tall ones forming a triangular shape from the top centre out to the sides. Those on short stems are placed close to the basket rim to add visual weight at the base of the decoration.

2 Larkspur and roses are arranged among the peonies, where they will conceal prettily the false stems. Small bunches of lavender, their stems cut short and bound with fine silver wire, are placed around the rim of the container to contrast with the neighbouring pale pink peonies and hydrangea heads.

THE SCENE IS SET

A Posy for a Guest

Emma has been a model baby, accepting pretty compliments with grace and charm. Her godparents have made their solemn pledges, and now the congregation of family and close friends has sauntered through the lych-gate and gathered for tea in the drawing-room.

Emma's mother chose to set the scene with rare simplicity, not with an impressive floral centrepiece but with a tiny posy set at each guest's place around the table.

Her choice of flowers is steeped in symbolism and delightfully appropriate to the occasion. Dainty rosebuds, in white and softest pink, signify 'beauty always new'. Clusters of baby-blue forget-me-nots symbolize remembrance and true love. Violas, according to one Victorian flower dictionary, stand for both innocence and modesty. Wild daisies gathered from the meadow behind the vicarage reinforce the sentiment; they, too, symbolize innocence.

The posy stems are bound with narrow bands of gossamer-fine ribbons, and each one is placed on a crisply folded white cotton napkin. Sugared almonds, a traditional token offered in celebration of a baptism, are held in circles of sugar-icing pink net tied dolly-bag style with satin ribbon.

A decorative napkin

1 Fold the napkin in half diagonally, and then bring up the left-hand and right-hand corners of the napkin to meet at the centre point.

2 Turn the now-square napkin over, and fold back the lower point to form a pointed 'cuff'. Fold under each side so that the sides of the completed fold are slightly angled outwards towards the top. You could if you wished place a single rose in the 'tuck' in the cuff.

A SPARKLING OCCASION

Wine Cups to Celebrate

The christening cake has been cut. Glasses have been raised aloft, and the toast to the infant drunk in the finest Champagne. As guests wander around the garden or gather in groups to exchange family news and gossip, they continue to luxuriate in the joyfulness of the occasion, and the wine flows. Now the mood of the moment is celebrated with a sparkling wine cup, ladled from an ornamental punch bowl and scattered with late-season's strawberries and rose petals. Raise your glasses again, ladies and gentlemen: here's to Emma, or Harriet, Edward, or Albert.

Rosemary-flower punch

SERVES 4

Typical of many Victorian sweet and sour fruit cups, this non-alcoholic punch combines the sugary-sweetness of apricot nectar with the 'kick' of ginger ale. Serve it to children at a christening party to make them feel grown-up.

❖ Put the long rosemary sprays in a small pan with the water and salt, bring slowly to the boil and simmer for 2 minutes. Leave to cool, then strain and chill.

❖ Pour the rosemary infusion into a large serving bowl and stir in the apricot nectar. Whisk well, then whisk in the lime juice. Just before serving, pour on the ginger ale. Decorate the punch with slices of lime and sprays of rosemary. Serve chilled.

YOU WILL NEED

❖ 2 15-cm (6-in) sprays of rosemary leaves and flowers
❖ 150 ml (5 fl oz) water
❖ pinch of salt
❖ 600 ml (1 pint) apricot nectar, chilled
❖ 150 ml (5 fl oz) lime juice, chilled
❖ 1 litre (1¾ pints) ginger ale, chilled
❖ 2 limes, thinly sliced
❖ short sprays of rosemary, to decorate

Hibiscus cup

YOU WILL NEED

* 75 ml (5 tbsp) Kirsch
* 750 ml (1¾ pints) hibiscus or other sweet flower tisane (see recipes for flower tisanes on pages 96 and 97), chilled
* 1 bottle sparkling white wine, chilled
* hibiscus petals or bergamot petals, to decorate

❖ Pour the Kirsch into a large serving bowl. Pour on the flower tisane and mix well. Just before serving, add the sparkling wine, and scatter the drink with flower petals. Serve chilled.

Rose-petal cup

YOU WILL NEED

* 60 ml (4 tbsp) caster sugar
* 60 ml (4 tbsp) brandy
* 60 ml (4 tbsp) Curaçao
* 1 bottle flower wine or other country wine, such as peach or strawberry, chilled
* 1 bottle sparkling white wine, chilled
* sliced strawberries, to decorate
* rose petals, to decorate

❖ Put the sugar into a large serving bowl and stir in the brandy and liqueur. Pour on the flower or country wine and, just before serving, the sparkling wine. Scatter with the sliced strawberries and rose petals and serve chilled.

HARVEST THANKSGIVING

Pot of Gold

The last of the harvest is gathered in. Orange-gold pumpkins are set out in rows to dry on flat sun-warmed rooftops and along the tops of red brick walls, and the lengthening shafts of sunlight seem to bounce back, dazzlingly, from crocks of gold. The leaves blowing this way and that beneath the trees are in a colourful kaleidoscope of russets, browns and golds that vie with the season's brightest flowers, and the air is abuzz with excitement.

The old barn is being made ready for the harvest thanksgiving supper, a red-letter day in the calendar of every country-loving Victorian family. Long branches of golden leaves are draped over doorways and windows; flowerheads and drying vegetables are strewn along the centre of trestle tables; and pots of flowers are set on the buffet tables and, casually, on upturned boxes on either side of the bays.

This is the time for joyful informality, a time to gather flowers and foliage from farmsteads and gardens, and bring in armfuls of golden rod and chrysanthemums, of chestnut-brown berberis foliage, speckled mahonia leaves and sun-bleached quaking grass. It is a time, too, to match the flower containers to the mood of the moment. Large well-worn earthenware crocks, old cider jars or wide-necked stone pickle jars would all be suitable. A block of soaked floral foam pushed into the neck of the container is an advantage Victorian flower arrangers did not have, and one that makes it possible to arrange the stems with studied informality to compose a design with a wayward look.

1 Create a tall oval shape in proportion to the container by arranging large dried or preserved leaves such as mahonia at a variety of levels, and at differing angles. Arrange short individual stems of spray chrysanthemums close to the rim.

2 Position tall, slender stems of golden rod among the tallest leaves, to define the height of the arrangement, then fill in with clusters of the flowers and more leaf sprays. Remember to keep the container topped up with water, so that the foam is constantly moist.

GIFT POSIES

A Lucky Harvest

Many Victorians living in the closely knit cereal-growing communities mastered the art of corn-dolly making. The practice of weaving and twisting hollow straws from the harvested wheat into symbolic 'maiden' and 'dolly' shapes pre-dates Christianity and was widespread a century or so ago. Farm labourers and children alike would sit in the cornfields and fashion designs unique to their locality, and display them or exchange them as symbols of good luck and fertility, in the hopes of a good harvest in the year to come.

Some people hung simple bunches of wheat on their doors and exchanged thanksgiving posies in gratitude for the fruitful harvest just gathered in and in hopes for a bountiful yield from that year's seedcorn.

In some regions it became the custom to embellish and decorate the bunches of wheat, adding bright seedheads and flame-coloured flowers, 'marygolds' and the last roses of summer among them.

The spirit of Thanksgiving

In the spirit of thanksgiving, what could be more delightful than a harvest posy to decorate a gift parcel, to be set at each place around the harvest-supper table, or to be arranged edge to edge around a vine-wreath base? The posies in the photograph were composed flat on a table.

Ears of wheat were arranged in a fan shape and covered by short lengths of brilliant orange Chinese lantern stems. Roses and marigolds, left in water until the last minute, were arranged at graduating levels, and the stems tied with shimmering coral-coloured ribbons.

PART FOUR

The
Flowers & Foliage of
Winter

Glossy evergreens woven into wreaths and garlands or arranged into kissing rings and winter posies; berry-bright fruits nestling among the foliage or piled pyramid high; colourful dried flowers composed into long-lasting table decorations and pretty bouquets, and seasonal flowers trimming a variety of gifts and parcels, these designs interpret the ways a Victorian lady decorated her home with the flowers and foliage of winter.

THE FLICKERING OF CANDLELIGHT

Advent Wreaths

The combination of glossy evergreens and lighted candles has its roots deeply planted in pagan times, when the dark winter months were enlivened by week-long festivals of fire and light and when, even amidst the revelry and riotous behaviour, candles symbolized cleansing and rebirth. The early Christian Church both adopted and adapted this symbolism in the form of Advent wreaths decorated with four candles, one to be lighted on each of the Sundays preceding Christmas day.

By Victorian times, when candle rings had become a significant feature of Christmas decorations around the home, the concept had evolved to include, among the evergreens, fresh and dried flowers, bon-bons, pieces of fruit and small parcels. Evergreens were carefully selected for their visual contrast, and Advent wreaths, the focus of attention on dining and side table, sideboard and windowsill, were further embellished with fulsome bows of velvet or satin ribbons.

The floral wreath

In the spirit of Victorian times, the wreath opposite is decorated with scented candles in deep shades of mulberry, cranberry and violet, and accented with an eye-catching bow in cranberry-coloured ribbon. In days gone by, such a wreath would have been built up on a moss-covered wire ring; this one is composed on a pre-formed ring of absorbent foam, soaked until it is saturated with water to provide a moisture source for the stems.

The ring base is closely covered with short sprays of juniper, eucalyptus and holly, and ivy with its clusters of jet-black berries. The natural highlights are provided by sprays of pink-flowering viburnum and icy-green hellebores. The candles are held in plastic candle-spikes, purpose-made to avoid splitting the foam, and the ribbon is wire-edged, which makes it easier to achieve a fully-rounded bow.

Golden evergreen ring

Composed on a small ring of dry stem-holding foam, the golden evergreen wreath is decorated with clusters of white tapers. Keep replacements at the ready, since these slender descendants of 'rush lights' have a short burning time. The foliage, a mixed palette of yellow and green, includes spiky juniper and golden cypress, glossy box and variegated eleagnus and holly. It is noticeable that the two variegated plants are reversed images of each other. The holly has green leaves tipped with yellow, and the yellow foliage is outlined with green.

Rich cranberry and mulberry colours
enhance this winter floral wreath

A LIGHT FOR ALL SEASONS

Shades of Summer

t the turn of the century, one of the brightest ways to keep alive the memory of warm summer days was the practical and pretty craft of decorating candles with pressed flowers and leaves. This was a family pastime, the perfect way to spend wintry evenings, and the designs could be as representational or as fanciful as mother and children chose to make them.

Candles in the warm, rich shades that were popular at that time, ruby, sapphire and amethyst, offer an ideal background for flower sprays, florets and petals in pastel tints from creamy white and silver-grey to buttercup yellow and sugar-almond pink, gathered perhaps on a country walk or on a visit to a flower-filled garden.

To carry out these designs you may choose to buy pillar candles in a variety of colours, or add a further dimension to the craft and make them yourself with paraffin wax, which was first introduced, as an extraction from crude oil, in the 1850s. You can dye the wax with soluble candle dyes, or paint white candles with acrylic paints dabbed on unevenly with a small stippling brush and then drizzled with paint in metallic gold.

Decorating the candles

Arranging pressed flowers to decorate candles is not a precise art, but one which offers scope for your creative talents and imagination. The medley of assorted flower sprays and florets arranged on the cranberry red candle is reminiscent of the way the flowers grew in Victorian times, in higgledy-piggledy profusion in cottage gardens and backyards. Such exuberance and freedom of expression is sure to enthrall generations of children, whilst the geometric arrangement of pink hydrangea florets on the blue candle is a fine example of a more restrained exercise in abstract art.

The two green candles exemplify the possibilities for creating contrasting designs. One candle is decorated with a composition of silver-leaved plants and snow-white miniature flowers which, although they were gathered and pressed on a summer's day, have much in common with the frosty, sparkling hedgerows of winter. The other candle, which was decorated on either side with a cut and pressed Chinese lantern seedpod, has a seasonal significance, too, in that the design is reminiscent of the Christmas star.

To decorate the candles, use clear papercraft glue. Arrange and rearrange the pressed materials until you find the pattern and the position pleasing, for even the most casual-looking designs need careful planning. Then spread a thin film of glue over the surface of the candle, press the flowers into place and wipe off the excess glue around the edges with a cotton bud. Hold a piece of paper over the pressed flowers and lightly run your fingers over it to press down the tips of the leaves and petals.

Your candles will be a lasting reminder of summers gone by. Until you choose to light them.

CENTRE OF ATTRACTION

Seasonal Colours

Glossy evergreens cut from the garden and dried flowers in subtle and seasonal colours; golden baubles and trailing tartan ribbons, and hand-rolled beeswax candles giving off the sweet scent of honey – this table arrangement combines many of the elements so beloved of the Victorian housewife.

She may have gathered deep, ruby-red hydrangea heads in late summer, just as they started to dry on the plant, and hung them in the boiler-house to dry, or stood them to dry, paradoxically, in a vase with a little clear, cold water. She may have bought the thistle-like carthamus flowers in a florists and dip-dyed them in mulberry or blackberry juice to achieve just the right shade of pinky red, and then selected mahonia leaves for their dramatic two-tone colouring, the green leaflets heavily spattered and speckled with red.

And she may have shown the children how easy and rewarding it is to roll the candles, starting with a sheet of waffle-textured beeswax and finishing, in a matter of moments, with slender candles for all to admire.

Creating the arrangement

Using present-day materials to create a Victorian-style design, the arrangement is composed on a block of soaked absorbent foam taped to a shallow dish. The candles are inserted in plastic spikes pressed into the foam, and the outline of the arrangement defined by the mahonia leaves, positioned to form a roughly rectangular shape. The holding materials are concealed by short sprays of red and green hydrangea florets, with the other materials nestling between them.

Making the candles

1 Place the rolled beeswax sheet on a piece of thick card and, using a rule as a guide, cut it with a sharp craft knife blade. Cut the sheet at right angles for candles with level tops, or at a slight diagonal for ones with a spiralled effect.

2 Place a length of wick along one edge of the sheet (the longer edge if you have cut it on the diagonal) and roll the wax to enclose it. Continue rolling the sheet tightly, and press along the edge to secure it.

THE HOLLY AND THE IVY

A Door Posy

The Victorian love of posies found expression at Christmastime in free-style wall and door decorations of holly, ivy and other evergreens tied together with exuberant ribbon bows. It may be no coincidence that this way of presenting long-lasting winter foliage has the closest links with the customs of the earliest times, when ancient peoples decorated their homes and places of worship with boughs of holly, ivy and mistletoe. They believed these evergreen plants had magical powers because they retained their leaves when other branches were bare, and myths, legends and superstitions grew up around evergreens. Many of these readily survived the transition into Christianity, and some enjoyed renewed status in Victorian times.

Holly's strong points

Holly with its vicious spikes and blood-red berries has long been seen as a means of ensuring personal protection. Young ladies in some regions of late nineteenth-century England edged their beds with holly boughs on Christmas Eve to ward off evil spirits. In Pennsylvania, in the United States, Native Americans pinned sprays of the prickly leaves to their clothes before going into battle.

Holly's protection against ill health had a long currency, and in the American state of North Carolina it became the custom to hand a sick child through a split cut in the trunk of a holly tree. The wound was then tightly bound and, as the timber healed, so the child's health would revive.

The superstitions linking holly first to the winter saturnalia and then to the Christmas festival are almost exclusively concerned with good luck, or the lack of it. It was considered the ultimate in ill fortune to cut down a holly tree, which may account for its proliferation even now in gardens and hedgerows, and bad luck to bring holly and ivy into the house before Christmas Eve. At the turn of the century in the north of England, some villagers placed a bunch of holly on their doorsteps in readiness for a 'lucky bird' to carry it inside on Christmas morning. If it could be contrived that the obliging first-footer was a dark-haired male, then luck was assured for the coming year.

A holly sprig for luck

Once the holly decorations had been put up, superstition dictated when and how they should be taken down. In some regions in Victorian England it was considered lucky to burn the fading foliage; while in other areas this was tantamount to asking for trouble. But there was, and still is, general agreement that the decorations should be taken down, not before and not after, but *on* Twelfth Night.

It was permissible, however, to retain a single sprig of holly to ensure good luck throughout the following

year, and some Victorians then used this to kindle the fire on which the Christmas pudding would be cooked. But when the pudding was served, set alight with brandy and ringed in dancing blue flames, the sprig of holly that adorned it must be thick with berries and plucked from one of the decorations.

The door posy opposite, with its layers of contrasting evergreens, contains many holly sprays that would glint and crackle a-top the Christmas pudding. The holly is layered with branches of Norwegian spruce (the traditional Christmas tree) and blue fir, juniper, rosemary, eucalyptus and ivy. Nestling among the evergreens, and toning with the ribbon bow, are stems of beautiful, bright orange Chinese lantern pods.

Make two loops for the bow,
leaving trailing ends.

Fasten the bow at the centre,
using fine thread.

LEAFY GARLANDS

A Seasonal Task

arlands of holly and ivy draped across mantelpieces, around tables and over doors; intertwined ivy stems outlining picture and mirror frames, and ribbons of evergreens, fruits, cones and gilded nuts wound around banisters and bedposts – the Victorians raised evergreen garlands and swags to a state of the high art.

In large English households it was the gardeners' seasonal task to fashion lengthy and elaborate garlands, the mixed foliage bound onto sturdy rope strung from end to end of the greenhouse. And it was their annual privilege to hang up these weighty decorations, out of sight of the children, on Christmas Eve.

Where garland length was concerned, no expense was spared on the other side of the Atlantic either. Records show that in 1898 Christmas shoppers were welcomed into New York department stores by a total of 64 km (40 mi) of evergreen garlands, constructed at a rate of 37 m (40 yd) per person per evening. These skilled workers, setting an enviable pace, bound 20-cm (8-in) sprays of holly and ivy to a thick rope core. Taking a leaf from their book, we have used this method, with evergreens cut to a similar length, to compose our festive, holiday garland.

Choice of materials

If evergreen garlands are to fulfill one of their earliest functions, to brighten homes and gladden hearts in the dark days of winter, both the foliage and the embellishments should be chosen with that in view. Long swathes of nearly black holly and ivy do little now, as in Victorian times, to add to the air of festivity, whereas variegated foliage tinged with cream and yellow, and clusters of gilded nuts catch every flicker of firelight and candlelight.

Wiring the cones

Wrap a medium-gauge stub wire (from florists) around each cone, and cross over and twist the two ends.

Wrap the wires around evergreen stems to attach them to the garland.

To add golden highlights, spray nuts with gold paint, leave them to dry, then glue them into clusters. Thread a stub wire through a gap between the nuts and attach them in a similar way.

Finish off the garland in true Victorian style, with a multiloop bow and long ribbon trails.

Composing the garland

Cut the evergreens to even lengths and form them into mixed bunches. Bind the first bunch so that the tips overlap one end of the rope, each successive one overlapping the one before.

RINGED WITH ROMANCE

Kissing Ring

When demure Victorian maidens and their diffident suitors shyly kissed under hoops of evergreens at Christmastime, their thoughts probably did not stray to the ancient origins of the kissing ring. They may or may not have known that these hanging decorations originated in pre-Christian times, when bringing holly and ivy indoors was thought to be a way of enticing the sprites of the forest to come inside too, and when entwining the two evergreen species together was a way of multiplying the 'good fairy' effect and setting the stage for romance.

For centuries after, the combination of holly and ivy in winter decorations was held to be a fertility symbol every bit as powerful as that of mistletoe, a plant that had once been seen as a protection against the elements of fire and water and later came to symbolize everlasting love.

By Victorian times, the respective symbolisms had become blurred, and it could be a hanging ball of holly, two criss-crossing hoops of holly and ivy or a simple bunch of mistletoe that provided the excuse for an innocent kiss.

Some romantic traditions persisted and others grew up around kissing rings. Young men had to pluck one of the white berries from the mistletoe every time they stole a kiss, and when there were no more berries left, the kissing had to stop. And marriageable young women saw to it that, of all the Christmas decorations, the mistletoe at least was burned on Twelfth Night. If this ritual was neglected, couples who had kissed under it might never marry.

To make the hanging ball

Cut short sprays of ivy – ones thick with clusters of glossy black berries are especially attractive – and, if possible, variegated holly. As a moisture source for the stems you can choose a large potato, as the Victorians did, or a pre-formed ball of absorbent stem-holding foam.

Thread wires through the top and twist them to form a loop. Suspend the ball on string while you cover it with alternating sprays of holly and ivy, packing them close together. When the ball is covered on all sides, and suitably romantic, decorate it as you will.

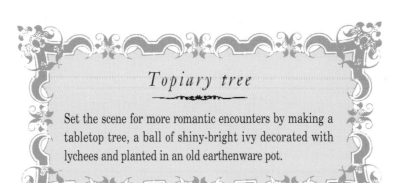

Topiary tree

Set the scene for more romantic encounters by making a
tabletop tree, a ball of shiny-bright ivy decorated with
lychees and planted in an old earthenware pot.

SEASONAL GREETINGS

Welcome Wreaths

In Victorian times, imposing entrances and cottage doorways alike were hung with colourful evergreen wreaths as a sign of welcome, and in continuance of a custom that pre-dates history. The circular shape, which has no end and no beginning, had long been held to symbolize hoped-for protection from evil spirits, as well as love, friendship, rebirth and even life itself. In a scaled-down version of these earlier beliefs, the Victorians hung their wreaths as a gesture of good-will to carol-singers taking their wassail bowls from door to door, to friends bearing seasonal greetings, and to every passer-by.

Composed on moss-covered wire rings, the wreaths, keeping faith with tradition, were tightly packed with sprays of holly and ivy. But then the Victorian flair for novelty took over, and the rings were decorated with toys and trinkets, beads and baubles, cones and cupids, fruit and flowers. Imagination had free rein.

Traditional door wreath

Two favourite decorative elements of the Victorian era – pine cones and small pieces of fruit – nestle among the evergreens in this traditional welcome wreath. The long-lasting foliage includes juniper and golden cypress, box, ivy and holly with thick clusters of berries.

The wreath base is a double copper-wire ring (from florists), covered with handfuls of moss bound in place with green garden twine. Bunches of evergreens are bound on in a similar way, the tips of each bunch positioned so that it covers the stem ends of the previous one.

The kumquats and cones are mounted on stub wires, in the way shown on page 152. The wire ends are pushed through the ring and bent flat on the reverse. The two-tone bow, in traditional Christmas colours, is wired in the centre and fixed at the top in a similar way.

Angel wreath

A woven stem ring, bought from florists, provides
the base for this green and gold welcome wreath.
Decorated at the top with a cherub ornament and at
the base with a richly coloured ribbon bow
looking like watered silk, the wreath is
steeped in Victorian tradition. Ivy leaves
sprayed with non-toxic gold metallic paint and
small gold-wrapped parcels catch every shaft of
sun- or lamp-light.

CHRISTMASTIME

A Fruitful Arrangement

The Victorians loved lavish displays of fruit and foliage and often used them in place of flowers to take centre stage on the dining table. Cascades of apples and pears, melons and peaches, grapes and figs spilling over the edge of three-tier glass or china pedestal stands, and pyramids of fruit piled precariously high on elegant silver dishes became a status symbol, admired as much for the seasonal achievements of the gardener as for the dramatic impact created by their varying shapes and glowing colours.

A new elegance

Table centre arrangements of this kind took on a new significance after the 1850s, when the Victorian mode of table service changed, and brought with it the opportunity, indeed the necessity, for a new elegance. No longer were all the used dishes left on the table until the end of the meal, with the consequent conflict of visual interest that caused. The new way of dining *à la Russe*, with each course cleared away in its turn, gave the aspiring hostess fresh incentive to compose creations of fruit, foliage and flowers that would be the talk and hopefully the envy of the neighbourhood.

Hothouse fruits were much sought after to complement the 'good keepers' such as apples and pears, and Victorian glasshouses were stoked up to provide the household with citrus fruits and table grapes throughout the winter.

In the spirit of this decorative expression of Victorian hospitality, it is as effective now as it was then to create a centrepiece of fruit, foliage and flowers. In the design opposite, the silver dish was fitted with a block of soaked absorbent stem-holding foam placed just off-centre and fixed to the base by means of a plastic 'frog' (from florists) and a dab of florists' clay.

A wire taken round the stem of the bunch of grapes and into the foam holds them in place, then a fan shape of fern leaves and scented geranium leaves is created around each side. A single red and green coleus leaf at the centre provides a background for a stem of pale green Singapore orchids.

Separated orchid flowers are arranged among the grapes, and piles of kumquats and lychees, apples and plums are built up on both sides. A scattering of holly-berry-bright cranberries take on a jewel-like quality, especially for Christmas.

PUNGENT POMANDERS

Christmas Tree Decorations

The image of Victorian children dancing around a fir tree laden with bon-bons and baubles, painted eggs and pretty flowers is so powerful that it is easy to forget that decorated trees had been a pivot of Christmas celebrations in the British royal household since 1800. This was when Queen Charlotte had a tree dressed at Windsor Castle to amuse the local children.

It was Queen Victoria's consort, Prince Albert, though, who saw the decorated tree as a symbol of family unity and happiness, and popularized a custom that had originated in his native Germany. There, in pagan times, people had hung decorations on bare branches to encourage the growth of new leaves. With the conversion to Christianity the practice switched from decorating deciduous trees to evergreen ones. The ancient fertility symbolism was dropped and ornaments became ever more elaborate and varied as time went by.

Glass tree baubles were introduced into Britain and the United States from Bohemia in the 1870s and were hung, glittering and fragile, beside blown eggshells decorated with beads, braids and flowers, pomanders, and tiny baskets filled with dried flower posies.

In the spirit of those times, and with more than a hint of nostalgia, we have chosen pungent clove oranges, or pomanders, for our tree ornaments, each one enhanced by a small bunch of roses and a ribbon bow. Mixing with the spicy oranges on the tree there are dried orange slices, the centre of each one covered with an aromatic star anise seedhead.

1 Choose thin-skinned oranges. Press whole cloves into the skin until the surface of the orange is completely covered. Place the oranges in a paper bag with a little ground orris root, and leave them in a warm place (such as an airing cupboard) for several weeks until they are thoroughly dry.

2 Cut short stems of miniature roses, gather them into small posies, and bind the stems with silver roll wire. Make a ribbon bow and stick it to the posy, then glue the flowers to the pomander. Hang the decoration on the tree with a colourless thread. Take the thread through the loop of the bow to secure it.

THE JOY OF GIVING

Presents Past

On Christmas Eve in 1832, five years before her accession, the young Princess Victoria went into the drawing-room at Kensington Palace in London and discovered to her surprise and delight that she had a Christmas tree and a pile of presents all to herself. Her joy was infectious, and the custom of exchanging Christmas gifts, little-known in England at the time, soon became fashionable.

By coincidence, the practice gained momentum on Victoria's marriage to Prince Albert who brought this delightful Yuletide custom, along with many others, from his native Germany. Spending their first Christmas together at Windsor Castle, the royal couple each had a tree set up in their respective rooms and surrounded each one with gifts as surprises for one another.

At this time, Christmas gifts were not always wrapped, but the element of surprise was soon to be enhanced by packing presents in boxes covered with coloured paper or cloth and tying them with multi-coloured ribbons.

Plain or fancy, our own Christmas present wrappings originate from Victoria's reign, as year after year we are able to experience the seasonal joy of giving.

Victorian-style wrappings

The parcels under the Christmas tree are wrapped in a selection of toning papers which, together, conform to the traditional colour scheme of red and green and set the scene for the floral trimmings.

A posy of glossy ivy leaves with clusters of black berries and a single dried red rose decorates a gift box wrapped in shiny black self-spotted paper circled by a thick red paper band. Two parcels covered in red paper and tied with ribbon and lace bands are romantically trimmed. One red parcel has a line of four white hyacinth florets, which in the Victorian language of flowers signify 'unobtrusive loveliness'. The other parcel is decorated with a single red rose tied to a spray of red and green mahonia leaves. Sprays of Christmas tree and a single poinsettia flower dramatically decorate the parcel wrapped with marbled paper, and a nosegay of box and dried red hydrangea florets completes the wrapping of the gold parcel.

SENTIMENTAL GIFTS

Winter Posies

Glistening snowflakes and sparkling frost, bright little snowdrops and other garden flowers treasured all the more, now, for their scarcity – winter has a special kind of romance that is there for all to see.

It is a special time for private romances too, for secret glances exchanged amid the flurry of the Christmas celebrations and for the reaffirmation of shared hopes in the year to come.

What better way to express these private feelings, and the joy of giving, than in a winter posy that is as pretty as it is sentimental.

Poinsettia posy

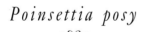

Bright and showy as they are, and with a brilliance that rivals even that of the holly berries, poinsettia flowers, or bracts as they are also known, have come to represent the very essence of traditional Christmas colour. A group of scarlet potted plants on the piano or a cluster of poinsettias planted in a deep china bowl make the boldest

The poinsettia posy carries a secret message of love.

of design statements in the complementary and seasonal colours of red and green.

Yet pluck a single flower from the plant and gather it together with toning blooms like pink pom-pom chrysanthemums and pink viburnum and the poinsettia becomes almost coquettish. The lace-tied posy is completed with wispy sprays of rosemary and a secret message of love carried in the almost hidden red rose.

The design of the circular posy is true to Victorian tradition.

Circular posy

Arrange it simply as a pretty composition of garden and greenhouse flowers or as a secret message to someone you love. Take the posy as a gift when you visit, or place it on the breakfast tray on Christmas morning.

The circular design is true to Victorian tradition, and the flower meanings an expression of something deeper than affection. There's rosemary for remembrance, and box for stoicism; pink chrysanthemums which, to those in the know, signify cheerfulness in adversity, and pink wax plant to indicate susceptibility to the charms of the recipient. The central feature of the posy, a red rose, speaks for itself – and for the donor.

New Year posy

The romance of winter, a wish for good fortune and hope in the future are all conveyed in this dainty pastel-coloured posy, which would make an unusual 'first-footing' gift. Arranged flat on a worktop in a cascade style, the posy contrasts prettily with the vibrant colours of the holiday decorations, like a private message whispered amidst a hubbub of general conversation.

The sprays of 'lucky white heather' that form the centre of the group are there to reinforce the 'hope' signified by the snowdrops. A gentle hint that all will, in the event, be well is given by the inclusion of the pale green hellebores whose reassuring message is 'a relief from anxiety'.

The New Year posy conveys hope and good fortune.

GILDING THE LILY

Flower-scented Honeys

he Victorians loved to gild the lily. Not content with savouring the characteristic flavours of honey gathered from fragrant country flowers and blossoms, they liked to strew pots of mild-tasting honey with more flowers and herbs, creating a never-ending permutation of complementary aromas.

As each season came round, the Victorians would fill their larder shelves with ever more sweetly scented varieties of honey – mimosa, jasmine and violet honeys in the spring; rose-petal, lavender and marjoram-flower honey in the summer; and, later in the year, jars of clear golden honey fragrant with the scent of evergreen herbs such as rosemary and bay, which would make lovely Christmas gifts.

Most flowers and herbs were simply infused with the honey while it heated, steeped and then discarded, but rose petals were more often ground to a coarse powder and stirred in, giving a more sweetly scented and cloudy preserve.

Flavoured honey

Choose any edible flowers or herbs, and any mild-tasting honey, for this steeping method.

❖ Place all the ingredients in a heatproof jar, cover it, and stand it in a pan with cold water to come almost to the top. Bring the water to the boil, remove the pan from the heat and leave it to cool.
❖ Leave the honey to steep for seven days, then gently reheat it and strain into a jar.

YOU WILL NEED

❖ about 6 small sprays of herbs such as rosemary, marjoram or bay, or 45–60 ml (3–4 tbsp) scented flower petals
❖ 1 long strip orange peel
❖ 15 ml (1 tbsp) orange juice
❖ 900 g (2 lb) clear honey

Rose-petal honey

Serve this in the Victorian manner, on toast or
toasted teacakes, muffins or scones.

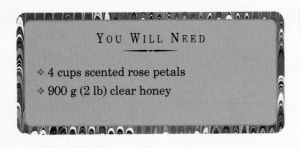

YOU WILL NEED

- ❖ 4 cups scented rose petals
- ❖ 900 g (2 lb) clear honey

❖ Wash and toss dry the rose petals if necessary, and
shred them coarsely in a blender or food processor.
❖ Gently heat the honey until it melts, pour it over the
rose petals and process for 2 to 3 seconds.
❖ Pour the honey into clean jars, cover with screw-on
lids and then with decorative covers.

SETTING THE TABLE

A Dainty Slipper

In Victorian times a table plan was not a pre-dinner-party reminder of who was to sit next to whom – though this was a matter of great social importance. Plans were drawn up and diagrams made of which dishes were to be placed where. During the first course, clear mock turtle soup scattered with white chrysanthemum petals might be 'removed' by salmon and lobster sauce. And later in the lengthy bill of fare the position occupied by a dish of ducklings might be taken up by raspberry cream ice decorated with rosebuds.

The centre of the table was always occupied by what Mrs Isabella Beeton, the celebrated Victorian author on household management, constantly referred to as 'a vase of flowers'; though on occasions (usually grand ones) an impressive display of fruit could be substituted.

Mrs Beeton advised her readers to exercise restraint when arranging flowers for the table, pointing out that an over-elaborate central display could prove a distraction from both the food and the conversation. She preferred the visual highlights to be distributed around the table setting, and encouraged the use of well laundered, lightly starched and exquisitely folded table napkins, pointing out that, 'whenever it is possible to do so, the appearance of the dinner table will be greatly improved by putting a flower or small bouquet in each napkin.'

The napkin folding designs on these and the following pages conform to Mrs Beeton's sound advice. The lady's slipper design, shown here, was especially popular to decorate the tables for weddings, christenings and other family festivals. It is worth noting that although the recognized size for a dinner napkin in Victorian times was 60 cm (24 in) square, the smaller and more decorative the napkin you use, the daintier the slipper will be.

1 Fold the napkin into four to make a small square, then fold it in half to make a triangle.

2 Fold over the two sides to meet vertically at the centre, then fold under and tuck in the two flaps.

3 Hold the napkin upright at the end where the flaps are tucked in and pull out each of the four corners in turn.

THE FLOWER BASKET

Elegant Folds

As Victorian hostesses vied with each other to produce the most elegantly folded table napkins in styles representing the *fleur-de-lys*, the lily, the palm leaf and the lotus blossom, frissons of excitement – even envy – must have rippled around the dinner tables.

Table napkins could be folded in a variety of ways so that they contained, in Mrs Beeton's words, 'a small dinner-roll, or a piece of bread cut thick, about three inches square . . .' Other folds were designed to contain or conceal a surprise gift for each guest, perhaps a parcel decorated with a single flower. When full-size dinner napkins were used, other styles of folding them were devised so that they could be placed in the centre of the table, holding a small glass dish and a nosegay of fresh and fragrant flowers. The design on these pages, known as the flower basket, is a place-setting version of this idea.

The enthusiastic advice Mrs Beeton gave to her readers on matters of the style and design of table napkin folds was tempered, helpfully, with practical words of warning.

'It must, however, be remembered that it is useless to attempt anything but the most simple forms unless the napkins have been slightly starched and smoothly ironed. In every case the folding must be exact, or the result will be slovenly or unsightly.' It is difficult to improve on or update such advice.

1 Fold the four corners of the napkin into the centre, then repeat the fold with the four 'new' corners.

2 Turn the napkin over, fold the four corners to the centre, and turn it over again.

3 Ease out the four corner flaps, lift up the four corners in the centre, and insert a flower or posy.

EVERLASTING COLOUR

Bright and Beautiful

Mulberry and mustard, purple and magenta, royal blue and cranberry – the deep, rich colours that were fashionable for furnishings in Victorian times were echoed in the lavish flower arrangements that decorated every room.

A rosewood wine table covered with a magenta chenille cloth might have been graced by a large shell holding a symmetrical flower display in tones from palest pink to deepest red. A butler's tray covered with a slubbed silk cloth might have doubled as a setting for a circular arrangement set on a tripod stand, and a side table might have been taken up by a decorative cake-stand supporting a pyramid of blooms in the most vibrant of primary colours.

We ourselves have not long emerged from a dark age when dried plant materials were characterized by their individual shapes and textures, but retained little of their brilliance; when browns, creams and faded-pink-velvet tones represented the pinnacle of our aspirations.

But with modern techniques, flowers can be dried in shafts of warm air or in heated desiccants so that they lose none of their former glory. As a result, they can continue to delight us through the winter and beyond in the vibrant colour combinations the Victorians loved.

The flower pyramid

The pyramid arrangement composed on a verdigris cake-stand is built around a curved block of dry stem-holding foam. Purple-dyed peonies alternate with cream roses around the rim, and then, layer by layer, there are clusters of hydrangea florets with red-dyed safflower (carthamus) flowers, deep red roses, a circlet of darkest blue air-dried larkspur, creamy white pearl everlasting, another hoop of roses, and a top-knot cascade of love-lies-bleeding, especially popular in the nineteenth century.

Position the arrangement where it will have pride of place, yet not be subjected to strong sunlight, which will cause the colours to fade prematurely.

FURNISHING POSIES

Delightful Decorations

The Victorians' love of posies extended far beyond lover's tokens and bridal flowers. Ladies liked to decorate their homes, too, with these delightful hand-arranged bunches, composing collections of dried flowers into round, sheaf or shower shapes to keep alive the scents and the memories of summer.

Small posies in the concentric-ring shape might have been placed beside a favourite fireside chair, a window seat or on a bedside table as tactile temptations to handle, sniff and twirl the ingredients. Flat-backed posies might have been hung on the wall above a bed-head or in an alcove, or placed on any otherwise unoccupied horizontal surface – on top of the piano, on library steps or on a sideboard.

Our interpretation of a Victorian furnishing posy contrasts the moody blues of dried cornflowers and larkspur with the romantic pinks of strawflowers and allium, and the cool greens of hydrangea and zinnias with the rich reds of peonies and roses.

1 Arrange the longest stems in a narrow fan shape on a worktop, then place seedheads and flowers in graduated lengths to follow the outline, the tallest ones in the centre, the shortest stems at the sides. Bind around the stems with florists' silver wire or raffia to hold them in place.

2 Add successive layers of flowers and seedheads, with ever-shorter stems, until there is a tight cluster of flowers – they might be hydrangea, sea lavender and strawflowers – close to the grip. Bind the stems securely, the tie them around with a bow made of two toning ribbons tied together.

PINK PERFECTION

In The Drawing-Room

Fresh or dried-flower posies were so much part of the Victorian drawing-room scene that special containers were manufactured to show them to their best advantage. These posy holders, made of silver, parcel gilt, porcelain or glass, were usually of a tripod design, some with a spring mechanism. It was the done thing to place a circular posy on the tea table or on a side table when tea was being served, and for an afternoon visitor to bring a posy as a thank-you token to her hostess. Such posies, whether they were composed of fresh or dried flowers, would usually be carefully colour co-ordinated, and regular visitors would take care to match their floral gift to the shades most favoured by the hostess.

When summer was over, tussie-mussies of flowers gathered from the garden gave way to equally beautiful compositions of roses and peonies, marigolds and zinnias, dried in dry sand or cornmeal. Although these desiccants offered less satisfying standards of colour retention than the chemicals used now, Victorian dried-flower posies had a definite, if slightly faded, charm.

Circular posy

The dried-flower posy is hand-arranged around a beautiful desiccant-dried peony. This central flower is encircled with dramatic bleached and dyed eucalyptus leaves (from florists) and then with cream roses. Clusters of hydrangea florets are twisted onto false wire stems to form the next ring, with outward-curving stems of mauve-dyed sea lavender forming the outer circle. A deep red rose is glued into the centre of the peony, and a gold paper doily pleated to form a decorative and protective collar. Trailing gossamer-fine ribbons take up the pink-into-purple colour theme.

SHADES OF NIGHT

Bedhead Posy

The shades of night have fallen fast. The bedside lamps are turned down low, bathing the room in a cosy orange glow, and are making only a faint spluttering sound. The floral patchwork quilt has been turned back, and the gleaming copper warming pan, long ago filled with hot, glowing coals, has been slid down between the sheets to warm the bed through.

With romance in the air, someone has crept into the room and hung a beribboned posy from one of the ornamental bedposts.

Pale cream and deep purple orchids, there are. In the Victorian language of flowers they signify beauty, and pay a tribute to a belle.

Bright yellow and fluffy mimosa there is, to show that spring is already on the horizon. Mimosa signifies, in Victorian terminology, sensitivity.

A tiny cluster of snowdrops, picked from a frosty, moonlit garden, hang their heads in pride. To Victorian ladies and their beaux they meant hope.

And long trails of ivy there are, symbolizing fidelity and marriage, and carrying the message, 'I cling to you.'

Composing the design

To create a flat cascading posy like this, place the trails of ivy, the largest single element in the design, flat on a worktop. Arrange a stem of Singapore orchids to entwine the ivy stems. Cut off individual orchid flowers from other stems and bind short lengths of silver roll wire to the stemlets. Bind these to the ivy stems, concealing the wires behind the leaves. Bind the mimosa sprays and the snowdrops into bunches and wire them into place.

Tie a length of gossamer ribbon around the stems, arrange the posy on the bedhead and shape the ribbon trails into gentle curves.

A pretty bedhead posy with trails of ivy
symbolizes fidelity and marriage.

TOGETHERNESS DRINKS

A Moment at Bedtime

are tree branches are groaning in the wind; rain is lashing the windows. In the safe, warm, pansy-velvet darkness indoors, it is the moment to share a bedtime drink.

Such nightcaps may be milk – or spirit – based. They may be soporific or reviving. And, if some old manuals are to be believed, they may also be aphrodisiacs.

Flowers have long had their part to play in enchantment foods and drink. Violets and valerian were said to have 'love-provoking powers', especially if they were gathered in the last quarter of the moon. Perhaps Cleopatra had good reason for having the ground before her scattered ankle-deep with rose petals. The wild orchid, known as satyrion, was used in the creation of the Greek and Roman aphrodisiac, *in excelsis*, and flower-scented honeys have a multi-cultural pedigree as an essential ingredient in togetherness drinks. Recipes for some favourite Victorian flower honeys are given on pages 166 and 167.

Rose-petal rummer

SERVES 2

A light and frothy blend of eggs and milk, spirits and honey.

❖ Beat the egg yolks with the sugar. Beat the egg whites separately until they form soft peaks, then lightly froth the egg yolks and whites together. Divide the mixture between two heatproof containers and pour on the rum and the brandy. Heat the honey and milk and slowly pour it over the egg mixture. Grate nutmeg on top and scatter each glass with rose petals.

YOU WILL NEED

❖ 2 eggs, separated
❖ 10 ml (2 tsp) caster sugar
❖ 10 ml (2 tsp) dark rum
❖ 10 ml (2 tsp) brandy
❖ 10 ml (2 tsp) honey, such as rosemary- or marjoram-scented
❖ 200 ml (4 fl oz) milk
❖ grated nutmeg
❖ rose petals

Rose-petal rummer

Mistletoe mull

SERVES 2

YOU WILL NEED

- 90 ml (6 tbsp) rose-petal honey
- 1 bottle Burgundy
- 1 stick cinnamon
- 2 cloves
- ½ orange, thinly sliced
- orchid petals or flowers

❖ Gently heat the honey, wine, cinnamon and cloves until just simmering. Do not allow the wine to boil. Remove it from the heat and leave to mull in a warm place for five minutes.

❖ Strain the wine into a heatproof jug or bowl, add the orange slices and scatter the orchid petals or flowers.

ACKNOWLEDGEMENTS

The publishers would like to thank the following for the contribution they have made to the designs photographed throughout the book:

GLYNISS FLORISTS
7 High Street, Halstead, Colchester, Essex CO9 2AS, tel (0787) 477177, *for assistance in obtaining fresh flowers for the Victorian-inspired arrangements and for the formal posies.*

NORFOLK LAVENDER LTD
Heacham, Norfolk PE31 1BR, tel (0485) 570384, fax (0485) 571176, *for the fresh lavender and some of the lavender preparations featured in the photographs.*

NORPAR FLOWERS
Navestock Hall, Navestock, Essex RM4 1HA, tel (0277) 374968, fax (0277) 372562, *for providing dried flowers and foliage, seedheads and grasses and exotic seed-pods and other imported materials.*

C. M. OFFREY & SONS LTD
Fir Tree Place, Church Road, Ashford, Middx TW15 2PH, tel (0784) 247281, fax (0784) 248597, *for the wide selection of ribbons.*

PRICES PATENT CANDLE CO LTD
110 York Road, Battersea, London SW11 3RU, tel (071) 228 2001, fax (071) 738 0197, *for so many of the candles featured in the photographs.*

ROYAL DOULTON LTD
Minton House, London Road, Stoke-on-Trent, Staffs ST4 7QD, tel (0782) 292292, fax (0782) 292099, *for providing so much of the tableware shown in the photographs.*

INDEX